Football Betting to Win

ALSO BY JACQUES BLACK
from Oldcastle Books

Spread Betting to Win

*The Moneyspinners: How Professional Gamblers
Beat the Casinos at their Own Game*

Football Betting to Win

Speculating on the Beautiful Game

Jacques Black

OLDCASTLE BOOKS

First published in the UK in 2000 by
Oldcastle Books, 18 Coleswood Road,
Harpenden, Herts, AL5 1EQ

www.highstakes.co.uk

Copyright © Jacques Black 2000

The right of Jacques Black to be identified as author of this work
has been asserted by him in accordance with the Copyright,
Designs & Patents Act 1988.

All rights reserved. No part of this book may be reproduced,
stored in or introduced into a retrieval system, or transmitted,
in any form or by any means (electronic, mechanical, photocopying,
recording or otherwise) without the written permission of the
publishers. Any person who does any unauthorised act in
relation to this publication may be liable to criminal prosecution
and civil claims for damages.

A CIP catalogue record for this book is available from the British
Library.

ISBN 1-84243-007-6

2 4 6 8 10 9 7 5 3 1

Typeset by Palimpsest Book Production Limited,
Polmont, Stirlingshire.
Printed by Omnia, Glasgow.

I am a part of all that I have met;
Yet all experience is an arch wherethro'
Gleams that untravell'd world, whose margin
   fades
For ever and for ever when I move.

– Alfred, Lord Tennyson, *Ulysses*

TABLE OF CONTENTS

**1 "DON'T MENTION THE WAR!":
   ENGLAND V. GERMANY, JUNE 17TH 2000   1**
   The build-up   1
   Match day   3
   The Game   5
   The Post-Mortem   7

**2 SHOUTING THE ODDS: A BRIEF HISTORY
   OF BOOKMAKING   10**
   From brokers to bookmakers   10
   1790: Ogden Shouts the Odds   11
   The 1940s: Las Vegas invents the line   13
   The 1980s: Spread Betting Arrives   14
   Conclusions   15

**3 "NOT WITH A BANG, BUT A WHIMPER":
   ENGLAND V. ROMANIA, JUNE 20TH 2000   17**
   The Game   17
   Tilting with the Tote   20

4 POOLS AND THE PUNTER   24
   The Mathematics of Accumulation   24
   How Football Pools are Organised   27
   A Potted History of the Pools   28

5 PLAYING THE POOLS   31
   The Treble Chance Pools   31
   How to play the Pools   33
   Conclusions   35

**6 SPREAD BETTING, THE POOLS AND FIXED
   ODDS COMPARED   37**
   Betting on the result   37
   Betting "in running"   38
   Closing bets in running   38
   Betting on the size of the discrepancy   39

Risk exposure	40
Tax efficiency	40
Convenience	41
Maximum payouts on winning bets	42
Average return per bet	42
The range of markets	43
Summing Up	43

7 EURO96 AND THE ART OF ARBITRAGE — 45
Arbitrage Defined	45
Arbitraging Euro96: The Set-up	46
Arbitraging Euro96: The Denouement	49
Goal scoring Times in Euro96	51
Conclusions	54

8 GOALS GALORE: WORLD CUP, FRANCE '98 — 56

9 EURO 2000: THE KNOCKOUT STAGES — 65
The Set-up	65
The Quarter-Finals	67
Holland v. Yugoslavia: the Second Half	68
The closing stages	70

10 PUNTING ON FOOTBALL SHARES — 74
Football Mania	74
The British Football Revolution	74
The rich get richer	77
The valuation of quoted football clubs	80
Boom turns to Bust: 1997–2000	82
Conclusions	84

11 SHOPPING AROUND — 86
Value Betting	86
Pre-season prices for the English Premiership in 2000/01	86
Converting odds to probabilities	88
Why shopping around it so important	90
Securing the information	93

12 FOOTBALL BETTING ONLINE — 96
The growth of online betting	96
The advantages of online gambling	97
Football information online	99
Conclusions	103

13 ONLINE GAMBLING SITES — 104
The High Street Bookmakers — 104
The Internet Bookmakers — 107
The Spread Firms — 109

14 FORECASTING FOOTBALL MATCHES — 112
An Atlantic Superleague? — 112
Forecasting Matches through Goal scoring Rates — 114
Recent form — 118
Elo type systems — 119

15 POINTS MEAN PRIZES — 122
Points differentials and the probability of home wins — 123
Points differentials and the probability of away wins — 126
Points differentials and the probability of draws — 129

16 THE PRIDE AND THE PASSION — 132
Psychological Momentum in Football — 132
The Fox and the Hare: Positive Motivational Factors — 136
Letdown and Exhaustion: Negative Motivational Factors — 138
Conclusions — 139

17 BOOKINGS AND BIASES IN GAMBLING BEHAVIOUR — 142
Why do people gamble? — 142
The Gambler's Fallacy — 144
The bookings index — 145

18 THE GOLDEN BOOT AND OTHER SPECIALITY MARKETS — 149
"That Petrol Emotion" and other propositions — 149
The Golden Boot 1994/95 — 151
The Golden Boot and Dynamic Duo, 2000/01 — 155

19 MEASURING SUCCESS — 158
How the Method Works — 159
Case 1 – The Sage of Omaha — 160
Case 2 – The Rugby Tipster — 164
Case 3 – The Blackjack Player — 165
Conclusions — 167

20 HOW TO WIN AT FOOTBALL BETTING — 169
Step 1: Developing a forecasting model — 169

Step 2: Testing the model 170
Step 3: Generating Prices 171
Step 4: Shopping Around 171
Step 5: Placing the Bet 172
Step 6: Record results and measure progress 173
Step 7: Evaluation 173

WHAT THE REVIEWERS SAID **175**

BIBLIOGRAPHY **181**

1

"Don't mention the War!": England v. Germany, June 17th 2000

The build-up

On June 17th 2000, England played Germany in a crucial match in Euro 2000.

The pre-match media build-up was dominated by memories of past clashes between the two adversaries. The long-suffering British public was treated to a rerun of the notorious "Don't mention the war!" episode of *Fawlty Towers*. We had to squirm in embarrassment once more at the sight of the young Paul Gascoigne bursting into tears when given the Yellow Card that would bar him from the 1990 World Cup Final. Worst of all were the reminders of the infamous red top headlines slurring Germany before the Euro96 clash, a nadir in the history of the British tabloid press.

In a predictable attempt to drum up business, the British bookies were entering into the spirit of things. *"Is it D-Day for England or will Germany keep the English pinned down under a barrage of attacks?"* trumpeted Sporting Index in their pre-match publicity. The firm opened for business with a "Behind Enemy Lines" index quote on the total number of offsides in the game with an opening spread 8.5–9.5. In even more questionable taste was their "Dad's Army" Index which awarded points for incidents in the game recalling catchphrases in the old BBC Second World War sitcom. You'll get the flavour of this index if I tell you that its components included "They don't like it up 'em" giving two points per foul by selected players and "You stupid boy", awarding ten points for an English Yellow Card, 25 points for a Red and 50 for an Own Goal. (David Beckham was to duly oblige in the "stupid boy" stakes).

The parallels with the War vested the game with far more importance than is merited by any sporting event. The simple facts were these. Within the context of the competition, this was a game that both teams needed to win to be confident of staying in the tournament. England had had a disastrous opening game. After going two goals up against Portugal, they had gone on to concede three goals to lose 3–2. No less an authority than Sir Alex Ferguson, writing in *The Sunday Times* on June 18th, put this result down to the tactical naivety of the England coach, Kevin Keegan. "I am not criticising Kevin for what occurred," he hastened to add. "His teams reflect his totally positive approach to the game. However, I couldn't see the sense in going hell-for-leather after a third goal. At 2–0, the match was won." At that point, Ferguson's approach would have been to shut up shop and play a tight defensive game.

But that was history on June 17th. There were two consolations for the English as they considered the outlook. First of all, Germany had done little better than they had in their opening game, being fortunate to escape with a 1–1 draw against Romania. And secondly, Portugal had done them an enormous favour by scoring a winning goal deep into injury time of their second round match against Romania. That result meant that Portugal were through to the quarter-finals – and also that England were in control of their own destiny. A victory against

Germany, followed by a draw with the Romanians, would be enough for England to qualify as runners-up in the group.

Truth to tell, whoever won the England–Germany game, most independent commentators gave little chance for either in actually winning the tournament. The German squad was well past its sell-by date. Most of their great players from the glory days of the early 1990s had retired, while their star striker, Oliver Bierhoff, was out injured. As for the English, most commentators felt that they simply didn't have enough quality players to pose a credible threat to World Cup champions France or to Holland, hosts and pre-tournament favourites.

But only time would tell.

Match day

After all the pre-match hype and speculation, it was almost a relief to get to the morning of the game itself. That Saturday morning I invested in a copy of the *Racing Post* for pre-match prices and hopefully some balanced analysis of the likely outcome. But even the *Post* seemed to have been carried away by the emotion of the occasion. "*At last – Germany are there for the taking*" screamed the back-page headlines.

As I studied the form over a cup of tea, the likely outcome did not seem quite as clear-cut as the headline suggested. England had last beaten their old adversaries 4–2 after extra time in the 1966 World Cup final, but that was now no more than a dim and distant memory. In 1970, England had squandered a 2–0 lead against Germany in the Mexico World Cup to lose 3–2 after extra time, the beginning of their long decline as a major force in world football. More painful defeats had followed, with the English losing on penalties to West Germany in the 1990 World Cup, and then repeating the experience at Euro96.

The simple question was whether England were good enough to overcome the legacy of history and their apparent psychological barrier and go on to beat the ageing German team over 90 minutes. I concluded that there was simply not enough evidence to bet on it with any confidence.

But were there any other positions that might generate a profit from the game? Leafing through the *Racing Post*, what impressed above all was the vast range of bets on offer – both traditional fixed odds and spreads. The array of prices was so bewildering that you would have needed the street savvy of an experienced options trader combined with the analytical skills of a rocket scientist to assess them thoroughly.

I had neither the time nor the expertise to complete a detailed analysis of all the prices on offer. So instead my task had to be the simpler one of asking the three fundamental questions which lie at the heart of any successful speculation:

- were any of the quoted prices fundamentally out of alignment with each other? If they were, there might be an opportunity for arbitraging, by playing different bookmakers off against each other;
- were any of the quoted prices out of line with the expected outcome of any event in the game, not just goals but corners or bookings? This was a tougher question to answer. Whereas you do not need to take any view yourself to exploit price variations between different bookmakers, to take an unhedged position you must have confidence that you are right and the bookie is wrong;
- what were the best prices on offer? Simply betting blindly with a single bookmaker is not a good idea. To maximise

profits you need to shop around to get the best prices on offer.

During Euro96, I had generated a substantial profit by arbitraging the prices offered by different bookmakers on the tournament, one of the most satisfying coups of my speculative career. But the bookmakers had tightened up their act since then, and there was no immediate promise of virtually risk-free profits on the England–Germany game. Nor was I sure enough of the two teams' strength to take an unhedged position on either of them.

One of the soundest speculative adages is: *when in doubt, do nowt*. So I sat on my hands and waited to see whether more profitable opportunities might be found by betting in running.

The Game

At 7.45 p.m. on a warm summer's evening, the game finally got underway at the Stade de Pays in Charleroi. During the opening quarter, the two teams played tentatively, approaching each other with a wary respect born of experience and reinforced by the knowledge that to concede an early goal would be disastrous.

More interesting than the sparring on the field was the battle going on off it. In the ITV's television studios, commentator Ron Atkinson was engaged in an heroic struggle with the English language, and as usual English was coming off a poor second. But in a rare moment of coherence on the half-hour, Big Ron made a comment with which it was difficult to disagree. "The signs are ominous," he commented as the Germans surged forward in attack. "And they're not a great side. This is as ordinary a German side as I've ever seen, but they've still got the organisation, still got the German method, still got a game plan. At the moment we don't know whether to stick or bust."

Certainly at that stage Germany seemed to be in control, and the spread on English supremacy looked generous. I took the fateful decision of selling the supremacy index at 0.2 for £100 a goal or £10 a point. This would generate a £20 profit if the game ended in a draw (£100 × 0.2), more if the Germans won.

But, as luck would have it, shortly afterwards the balance of the game swung after a superb Michael Owen header was only kept out by an outstanding save. It seemed to galvanise the English into action, and they dominated the last ten minutes of the first half. Half-time came as a relief for the Germans – and for me.

It was not to last long. Eight minutes into the second half, the deadlock was broken. Almost inevitably, it was through a Beckham cross, curving duplicitously behind the stranded German defence, connecting with a Shearer header at the back post that gave the goalkeeper no chance.

And that was more or less that. Perhaps more streetwise after their defeat by Portugal, the English were content to defend their 1–0 lead. Gerrard was brought on for Owen to reinforce the defence, and the Germans never showed any sign of breaking it down. At the end of the game, there was almost a sense of anti-climax that a game that started with such a huge build-up should have evolved so tamely.

I lost £80.

The Post-Mortem

The betting market had not been much livelier than the game. The bread-and-butter supremacy market, which had opened with a quote of 0.2–0.5 England over Germany, had moved slowly downwards as the clock ran on to half-time, before bumping up to 0.9–1.1 after Shearer's goal early in the second half put England 1–0 up. It stayed at that level through to the full-time make-up of 1. In other words, for the last half-hour of the game, you could have "sold" England's winning margin at 0.9, or "bought" it at 1.1. Either way, the punters would have lost money and the spread firms would have made 0.1 times their bet per goal.

The evolution of the supremacy index through the game is shown in Figure 1.1, which reveals that it barely moved apart from the shot in the arm injected by the Shearer goal.

Figure 1.1
Midpoint of the Supremacy Index in the England v Germany game

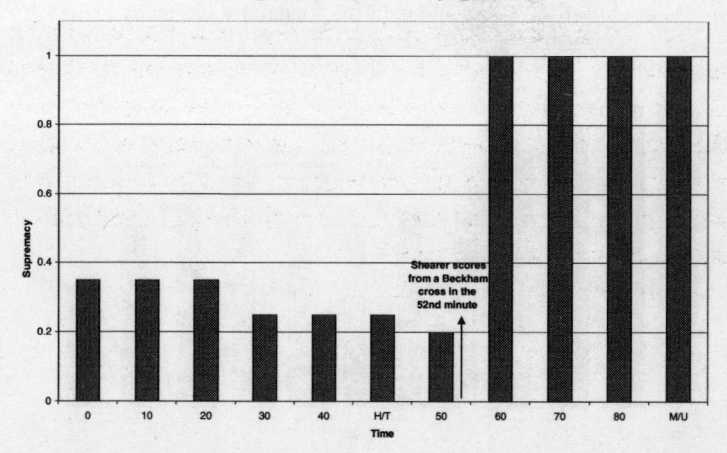

Source: Sporting Index live quotes on ITV Teletext, June 17th 2000

The Total Goals spread, quoted on the total number of goals scored during the game, was hardly more exciting. The opening quote of 2.4–2.7 gradually moved downwards until Shearer scored, and then it was adjusted upwards before resuming its downward path to expiry, as shown in Figure 1.2.

Figure 1.2 reveals that, during the phases of play in which no goals were scored, the Goals Index moved down by between 0.2 and 0.3 every 10 minutes. One suspects that there was very little for the market maker to do. The adjustment was automatic, with the index in any minute approximately equivalent to the number of goals scored to date plus (the opening quote multiplied by the number of minutes remaining divided by 90). Applying this formula, you can see that, with an opening price of 2.55 goals, the midpoint quote after 30 minutes would be 2.55 × 60/90, or 1.7. In fact, the actual quote on the half-hour was just a shade higher than this, reflecting the fact that on average more goals are scored in the second half than the first.

Figure 1.2

Midpoint of the Goals Index in the England v Germany game

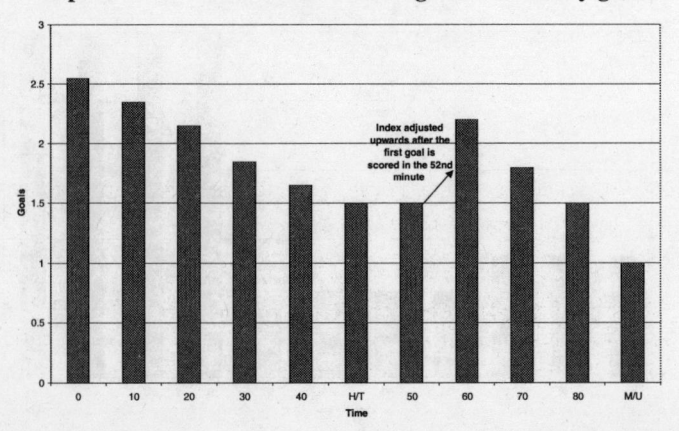

Source: Sporting Index live quotes on ITV Teletext, June 17th 2000

Overall, a low-scoring game such as the England-Germany clash is easy money for the spread firms, who need to do little more than make sure their accounts are in order and tot up the cash at the end.

It was tougher for the fixed odds boys, who had typically offered pre-match odds against England of around 6/4, with Germany quoted at 13/8 and the Draw 2/1. With most of the patriotic punters' money going on England, the fixed odds bookies probably made little if any profit on the game. But this would only represent a temporary blip in several centuries of profitable business for them.

2

Shouting the Odds: A Brief History of Bookmaking

From brokers to bookmakers

Gambling is as old as human history, and bookmaking is not far behind.

The earliest bookies were no more than honest brokers who held the stakes put up by two gamblers until the final outcome of their bet was known. In medieval times, Lords of the Manor who owned fast horses might propose match races against their neighbours. To make the event more interesting, the two owners would bet on the outcome. Once stakes were agreed, they would be entrusted to a reputable third party. In return for providing this service, the stakeholder customarily received a percentage of the winnings as a tip.

Over time, what started out as a friendly wager between two noblemen often developed into a major social event drawing big crowds from the villages of the two protagonists. Invariably some of the spectators also wanted to bet on the outcome, and so the role of the stakeholder evolved to accepting their bets as well. But at first the stakeholder would only be willing to hold a wager if he could find someone else willing to back the other horse for the same amount.

But as time went on, it became clear that, if a stakeholder was only willing to accept matched bets, the procedure could take some time. It would also result in the refusal of any bets that could not be matched. So in due course stakeholders came forward who were willing to accept bets without necessarily balancing their books. This new breed of risk takers gradually displaced the "honest brokers", and they soon became known as "bookmakers" because they were prepared to make a book on the race.

With the basic infrastructure of horseracing in place, and a market of spectators willing to put hard cash into action on the outcome, courses began to be developed specifically for horse races. Ad hoc two-horse races held when one landowner challenged another evolved into a regular calendar of races often coinciding with major market days and holidays. The races expanded from contests between two horses to larger events involving three or more horses.

In the early multi-horse races, bookmakers were able to maintain the principle of match races by identifying the strongest horse in the field and pitting it against all the others for betting purposes. But betting one horse against the field gave rise to a major problem. It became more and more difficult for bookmakers to achieve an even balance of bets between the two sides. If one horse was clearly superior, few punters were willing to back the field; but if the race attracted a number of horses of similar quality, the opposite was true. Either way, the bookmaker could be exposed to significant losses.

1790: Ogden Shouts the Odds

The crucial moment when the traditional stakeholder was transformed into a fully-fledged bookmaker is generally dated back to the Newmarket racecourse in the year 1790. In that year, a Lancastrian named William Ogden became the first man on record to shout the odds on every horse in a featured race. Ogden rapidly won business and became the most popular bet taker on the course. Anyone who had a particular interest in one of the field horses would bet with Ogden rather than backing the Field against the Favourite with one of the traditional market makers, because Ogden's payouts on named horses in the Field were invariably better. Traditional bookmakers might offer odds of 5/6 on the Field, whereas Ogden might offer 3/1 against each of the four horses making up the Field.

But the original concept of the match bet has not become obsolete. It remains the foundation of sports betting to this day. Although its importance in horse racing has progressively diminished because it is not appropriate for contests involving many participants, this is not true of football games that involve just two teams. So even today, a bookmaker might be quite happy to quote 5/6 on each team to go through in an evenly matched FA Cup clash. For league games, the situation is complicated by the fact that almost a third of all games end in draws, but the basic concept still applies.

However, the match bet in its simplest form can really only be applied between teams of roughly equal strength. Where there is a gross mismatch – for example in an Italy v Liechtenstein international – any bookmaker offering roughly equivalent odds on the two sides would quickly be overwhelmed by bets on the favourite, and would go bankrupt when Italy won at a canter. But the alternative of adjusting the odds to reflect the true supremacy of the favourite also has its limitations. There would be few takers if a bookie offered odds of 1/150 on Italy – requiring the punter to bet £150 to win just £1. Business would simply dry up.

The 1940s: Las Vegas invents the line

William Ogden was a bookmaker in the original sense of the word, because he was prepared to "make a book" on a race ahead of bets being placed. He therefore accepted risks. If he did not react properly to the flow of money by adjusting his prices to reflect the flow of betting on different horses, his book would become unbalanced, exposing him to losses if particular horses won.

A century and a half after Ogden, Las Vegas bookmakers sought to reduce their risk on sporting events by introducing the "point spread" in an effort to equalise the flow money between two teams. Originally applied to American Football, it rapidly became the standard method for equalising the flow of money on other events.

Whereas Ogden had to make his own mind up about the relative chances of different horses in a race, and then had to be prepared to put his money where his mouth was, many of his American successors do neither. They take their prices from the line set by independent linemakers. If the flow of funds is not balanced on both sides of the line, they can hedge their exposure by placing bets with other bookmakers. If there is an overwhelming flow of funds to one side of the line within the market as a whole, then the line will be adjusted upwards or downwards to reflect it.

In the USA, for many years bookmakers took their point spread predicting the margin of supremacy in points of the Favourite over the Underdog in American Football games, from Bob Martin. Martin was the leading linemaker in Las Vegas for twenty years until his retirement after the 1982 Super Bowl. Michael Roxborough, who opened his Las Vegas Sports Consultants business in the same year in which Martin retired, succeeded him as the market leader. As its name suggests, Roxborough's business is primarily a consultancy rather than a bookmaking operation. Roxborough draws on the research and opinions of many handicappers around the USA to arrive at his point spread for a particular game, and then sells these forecasts to bookmaking firms in return for payment. The success of his business ultimately depends on the confidence his clients have in his forecasts, which in turn depends on their accuracy. Clearly the results in any single game could fluctuate either side of Roxborough's point spread, but provided these fluctuations are random and that overall the results are close to his pre-match forecasts, his clients in the bookmaking fraternity will make money by using them as a basis for their own prices.

The 1980s: Spread Betting Arrives

The next extension to the match bet concept came with the arrival of spread betting in the UK. First developed by Jonathan Sparke through his firm City Index, it sought to apply risk management techniques first developed in the financial markets to sporting events.

In spread betting, the bookmaker neither takes nor lays odds on a particular event, but rather establishes an index in which a different price is quoted for selling and for buying. For example, the opening quote for the supremacy of England over Germany in their Euro 2000 match was 0.2–0.5. In other words, punters could "sell" England's supremacy at 0.2 or "buy" it at 0.5. Provided that the spread firm takes roughly the same number of buying as selling orders, it will make money no matter what the final result. The index firm quoting the spread has no interest in the outcome of the game; it earns its return through the "spread" or difference between the buying and selling prices.

To see how this is achieved, consider the case of a Total Goals index for a particular game. Spread bookmakers typically open this index with a quote of around 2.4 to 2.7. In other words, someone wishing to take a position on the number of goals scored during the game could *sell* goals to the index firm at 2.4 or *buy* them at 2.7. So someone who thought that a particular match would be low scoring might sell goals at £50 a goal, or at £5 a point, where a point is defined as a tenth of a goal. Conversely, someone who thought that the match would be high scoring might buy goals at £50 each. If the final result of the match were 1–1, the seller would win (2.4–2.0) × £50, or £20; while the buyer would lose (2.7–2.0) × £50, or £35. The spread bookmaker would make an overall profit of £15, or (2.7–2.4) × £50, on the two positions. In fact, the bookmaker would *always* make a profit of £15, no matter how many goals were scored.

Conclusions

The history of bookmaking is essentially one of risk management. Bookmakers offer a service of taking bets on racing and sporting events, and expect to earn a modest return for this service. If they have to accept significant risk as well, as William Ogden did, they will charge an additional premium for this risk. The traditional High Street bookmakers who have followed in Ogden's footsteps are exposed to risk in this way. But over the past half-century, two major innovations have occurred in the pointspread and index betting, and both have had the effect of reducing the bookmaker's risk exposure.

So the wheel has turned full circle. The spread bookmakers

of the 21st century more closely resemble the early stakeholders of Medieval England than the bookmakers of the 19th and 20th centuries who followed Ogden in offering fixed odds. The new breed of index bookmakers seek to equalise the flow of funds between buyers and sellers, run balanced books and expose themselves to as little risk as possible.

This is not necessarily bad news for the punter. By carefully managing their risks, the index firms can offer finer prices and better value than their fixed odds brethren. But it does mean that the successful speculator is no longer someone who can outwit the bookie. The challenge now is to be smarter than the rest of the gambling market.

3

"Not with a bang, but a whimper": England v. Romania, June 20th 2000

The Game

With victory over Germany under their belts, all England needed to do to qualify for the quarter-finals of Euro 2000 was to secure a draw against Romania. For Romania, nothing less than outright victory would suffice, and even then they needed Portugal to at least draw against Germany if they were to get through.

The very different objectives of the two sides were evident from the outset. Romania came out of the traps a lot faster than the English, who seemed content to play a waiting game, slowing the play down and seeking to retain possession. But they paid the penalty for their unadventurous approach when they conceded a soft goal in off the far post in the 23rd minute.

As if shocked by being the goal down, England at last began to play. But it has to be said that there was a distinct lack of imagination or flair in their game plan. No matter; with a more positive approach, their luck changed when Ince was brought down in the penalty area five minutes before half-time, and Shearer made no mistake from the penalty spot. Then, on the stroke of half-time, a moment of individual flair increased their lead. A speculative long ball through behind the Romanian defence, a devastating turn of pace from Michael Owen to beat the diving Romanian goalkeeper, clinical finishing, and England were 2–1 ahead.

"You can never write off the English," opined BBC pundit Alan Hansen during the half-time interval, "they are mentally so tough, they never give up." He reinforced his views with a few less than complimentary remarks about Eastern European players, who were apparently made of more pliable material than the doughty Anglo-Saxons.

Watching the drama unfold on the television in the peace and quiet of my sitting-room, I wondered where on earth otherwise intelligent commentators such as Hansen dredge up the gibberish with which they pepper their observations on occasions such as these. If you're 1–0 down less than half an hour into a 90-minute game, it does not require "mental toughness" to continue playing with a degree of discipline and self belief, just the basic experience of knowing that, in such a situation, the game is far from lost and there is absolutely no point in lying down. Nor, if you are unfortunate enough to lose a goal just before half-time, does it mean that you are "mentally weak". It could just mean that you were unlucky, momentarily lost concentration, or were the victims of a moment of individual genius – or some combination of all three, as I suspect was the case with Romania.

Whatever the truth of the matter, rarely can the fallacies of a so-called expert have been shown up quite so cruelly as in the case of Alan Hansen's half-time remarks.

Obviously, I have no idea what England's manager said to his team at half-time. But the way they went out into the second half would suggest that it could have been something like "all right lads, we're a goal up, so all we have to do is sit on the ball and watch the clock wind down." Had Kevin Keegan been stung by Sir Alex Ferguson's criticism of his tactics in the opening game against Portugal? Had he been irked by the remarks of Manchester Utd's coach, as he had on a notorious occasion a few seasons previously, when he had exploded into an over-emotional tirade on television as Man U inexorably overhauled his Newcastle Utd side in the closing stages of the Premier League? And was he once more reacting to Ferguson's comments to the detriment of the team he managed?

Whatever the truth of the matter, England went out into the second half showing every sign of being content to sit on their lead, and were duly punished when Romania equalised barely three minutes into the half.

But even at 2–2, there was a certain lack of urgency about England's play. Having ridden out the storm, they seemed content to revert to their unadventurous game plan, leaving it up to the men in yellow to try and force the game. Of course, it was true that a draw would be enough to see England through, but with the team playing deep – usually having nine men behind the ball – they were inviting the Romanians to attack. With nothing to lose, the Romanian team duly took up the challenge, and only solid goalkeeping from Nigel Martyn kept England safe.

But the English strategy of playing for a draw became increasingly risky as the game wore on. The problem was that, if Romania were to score, there would not be enough time for England to recover the situation. So any mistake could be fatal.

Remarkably, with an hour on the clock and the score standing at 2–2, the Tote were still offering odds of 3/1 against a Romanian victory, with England at 7/4 and the draw at even money. Irritated by the xenophobic comments of the TV pundits, I swallowed hard and bet £100 on a Romanian victory.

But as the clock ran down, it looked like being my second losing bet of Euro 2000. "What we have, we hold. We've got the point we need. That's the attitude of the England team," reported BBC commentator Barry Davies about ten minutes from the end. It was an entirely accurate assessment. But in the circumstances, it was also an extremely high risk strategy.

And so it proved. Three minutes from the end of ordinary time, an appallingly clumsy tackle by Phil Neville conceded a penalty that Romania duly converted to give them a 3–2 lead and an unexpected victory.

With the Portuguese victorious in the evening's other game against Germany, the result meant that Romania were through to the quarter-finals and both England and Germany were eliminated. So the experts were proved right. Neither of these two traditionally strong football nations had been good enough to get through to the last eight. England's spiritless exit brought to mind nothing so much as the closing words of T.S. Eliot's *The Hollow Men*,

> *This is the way the world ends*
> *Not with a bang but a whimper.*

Tilting with the Tote

It was difficult to disagree with the immediate post match assessment of England coach Kevin Keegan, who conceded that his side had simply not exercised sufficient control over the game to get away with a result.

"With ten minutes to go, we were shipping water all over the place," he commented. "If you keep giving away the ball, instead of controlling and passing it, you are leaving yourself with too much to do." In the end, England's passive approach to the match had handed the initiative to Romania, and most of the post-match media analysis concluded that the Romanians deserved their victory.

But what is striking is that this was not reflected at all in the Supremacy prices quoted by the spread firms, or the fixed odds quoted by the Tote during the running. While the odds swayed backwards and forwards as goals were scored, they consistently favoured England except for the 18-minute period in the first half when Romania enjoyed a 1–0 lead.

Figure 3.1 shows the Tote's prices at ten-minute intervals during the game, converting the Tote odds into percentage probabilities: so that, for example, the 3–1 price offered against a Romanian victory after 60 minutes converts into a 25% win probability on the graph.

The graph tells the story of how the game evolved as seen by the Tote. The pre-match quote of 10/11 on an England win, 9/4 against the draw and 12/5 against Romania changed dramatically after Romania went into the lead in the 23rd minute. On the half-hour, the price offered on a Romanian win was 2/3 on. But this changed when England equalised and then shifted decisively towards the English when they went into the lead at half time. At the interval, the odds on an England victory were as short as 5/7 on, implying that, for a bet on England to be worthwhile at that point, you would have had to assess England's true chance of victory as more than 70%, and more like 80% once betting tax is taken into account. How many people at half-time would have risked £4 on England to win just £1? Only those seduced by Alan Hansen's fallacious analysis, I would suggest.

When Romania equalised early in the second half, the odds against England lengthened to 3/2, implying a 40% chance of victory, slightly less than the odds against a draw at 9/4 (44.4%). As the clock ran down and the scores remained level, the odds against a draw shortened. By the 70th minute, the Tote was offering a draw at just 8/11 on.

Figure 3.1
Percentage probabilities of an England Win, Draw and a Romania Win implied by odds quoted by the Tote at intervals during the game

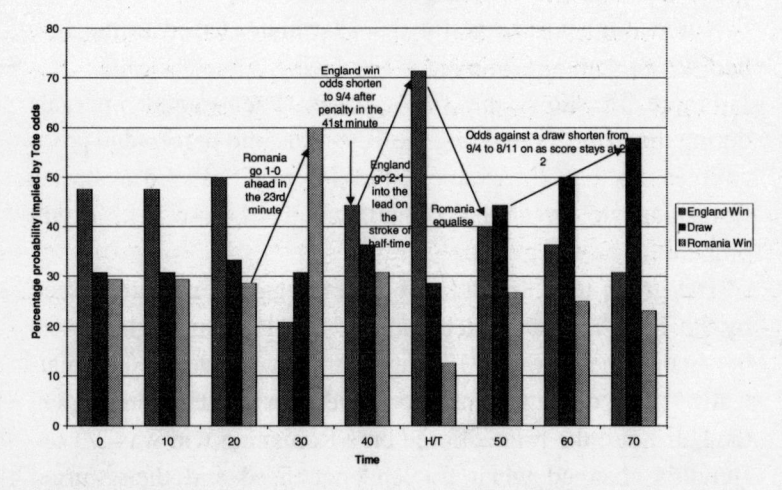

[Bar chart showing percentage probabilities implied by Tote odds over time (0, 10, 20, 30, 40, H/T, 50, 60, 70 minutes) for England Win, Draw, and Romania Win. Annotations: "Romania go 1-0 ahead in the 23rd minute"; "England win odds shorten to 9/4 after penalty in the 41st minute"; "England go 2-1 into the lead on the stroke of half-time"; "Romania equalise"; "Odds against a draw shorten from 9/4 to 8/11 as score stays at 2-2".]

Source: Tote live quotes on ITV Teletext, June 20th 2000. The Tote closed its book on the game after 70 minutes.

Figure 3.1 shows how suddenly and dramatically prices can alter over the course of the game in response to shifting fortunes. But it also reveals how far prices can diverge from the pattern of play – at least as described by independent commentators and even the England manager after the game was over! When I placed a bet with the scores level after 60 minutes, Romania clearly held the initiative on the run of play, yet they were quoted as 3/1 against compared to England's 7/4, with the draw offered at even money. These odds must have reflected the overwhelming weight of money on England, and hence the Tote's potential liabilities in the event of an English victory.

Clearly, fortunes could have swung back the other way, as

they had in the England-Germany game three days earlier, in which case I would have been left nursing a loss of £100. As it was, Romania's winning goal three minutes from the end generated a profit of £300.

The wider moral of the story is that better value is generally secured by betting against the crowd rather than with it – and ignoring the often partisan comments of TV pundits!

4

Pools and the Punter

The Mathematics of Accumulation

Single bets on the outcome of football games date back as long as the game itself. In his book *From Prohibition to Regulation*, David Dixon reports that the formation of the English Football League in 1888 "attracted the interest of bookmakers and football betting became a considerable part of their business, providing a useful substitute outside the flat racing season."

But it wasn't long before the activities of the bookmakers attracted the reciprocal interest of the Football League and the government, who soon banned betting on individual matches because they feared that match fixing might bring the game into disrepute. It was not until 1990 that this prohibition was relaxed and single bets permitted on live televised matches.

The consequence of the ban was that fixed odds business throughout the twentieth century was almost exclusively in combination betting, where gamblers had to forecast the results of a number of different matches on the same coupon. Even today, many High Street bookmakers accept only trebles and upwards on non-televised games, so that the gambler has to make a minimum of three separate selections. Some even insist that, for Home Wins, there must be a minimum of *five* selections if the bet features games outside the Premiership, Division One and the Scottish Premier League!

From the gambler's viewpoint, the only advantage of combination betting over single bets is that they offer the prospect of a bigger payout if things go well. In his book *Gambling on Goals: a century of football betting*, Graham Sharpe reports that in 1910 one London bookmaking firm, Pattmans, quoted 8/1 against six home wins and 100/1 about four draws. These odds were not far from those offered by Sharpe's own firm, William Hill, in 1997, at 17/2 against six homes and 104/1 on four draws. Certainly a payout of more that £100 on a £1 winning bet on four draws looks tempting. By way of comparison, if you placed four single bets on four games ending in a draw at odds of, say, 9/4 each, the winning payout if all four results came in would be just £9 for every £1 wagered.

The reason for the much higher payout on combinations and permutations of several bets is that the gambler's stake is increased by every winning bet. A similar effect could be achieved by simply ploughing back each winning bet in a series of single bets. To see this, let's consider what would happen if you follow the advice of Rudyard Kipling, and "make one heap of all your winnings, and risk it all on one turn of pitch-and-toss". If all four bets are on draws, and the odds are 9/4 against each one, then should all four win the cumulative effect would be:

○ a return of £3.25 from the first bet – a win of £2.25 and the returned stake of £1;
○ the second win would increase the stake to £10.56, with a win of £7.31 to add to the £3.25 stake;
○ the third win would further increase the stake to £34.33; and

○ after the fourth, the total return would amount to £111.56, or a net win of £110.56 on the stake of £1!.

Of course, the problem is that, if any of the individual bets lose, the entire sequence loses. So even if three out of the four bets are successful, we would be wiped out, whereas with this success ratio we would make steady small profits if we stuck to singles.

But most gamblers prefer occasional big wins to grinding out a series of small returns. And until very recently the imposition of penal rates of betting tax in the UK meant that anyone seeking to grind out a living in this way would almost certainly have ended up going slowly broke.

To see why, consider the career of Phil Bull, one of the most successful professional gamblers Britain produced in the twentieth century. According to an analysis of his betting record provided in *Bull: The Biography*, by Howard Wright, he amassed a profit of £300,000 from betting on horseracing between the 1940s and 1970s, equivalent to £4.6 million in 1995 prices. He made profits in 24 of these years and incurred losses in only 8. He achieved these results by applying his knowledge of statistics and mathematics to develop the Timeform system, which provided a scientific method for ranking the comparative strength of racehorses.

But the point is this: impressive as Bull's gains were in *absolute* terms, they represented a percentage margin of less than 10% of the amount of money he put into action. When betting tax was introduced, most of Bull's margin was wiped out. In 1977, Bull faced a 4% tax even when betting on course. At the end of that year, he complained that his records for 1977 indicated that he had won a gross amount of about £37,000, of which £17,000 had disappeared in betting taxes.

The fact that a model professional like Phil Bull could be

forced into retirement by the introduction of a 4% on-course betting levy demonstrates that even an apparently small reduction in the margin earned on speculative activities can have a dramatic impact on their profitability.

In some respects, the opportunities open to a professional gambler in the early twenty-first century are superior to those which prevailed when Bull retired. The 4% on-course betting duty has been abolished. It is also possible to bet tax-free through Channel Islands bookmakers and, increasingly, over the Internet. The off-course bookmaking market is also highly competitive, and the development of index betting (which did not exist in Bull's day) offers a range of new possibilities to speculators.

Yet, even with these advances, most bets on horse races and football games are still placed through the High Street bookmaking shops, where winning bets are taxed heavily. Once the effect of the tax is taken into account, accumulator bets on which tax is paid just once start to become more attractive than a series of single bets each taxed separately.

How Football Pools are Organised

Once the combined impact of tax and the possibility of huge payouts are taken into account, the attractions of the pools become obvious. The football pools are so called because all moneys staked are placed into a pool. The organisers take a cut from the pool in payment for their services in running it, and the remainder is divided amongst the winners.

Although the winners do not know how much they will win in advance – as it depends on the number of participants, the total amount paid into the pool, and, crucially, the number of winning forecasts – in a big pool, the size of the win can be many thousands of times the value of the initial stake. For example, in February 1994, one gambler won £2.25 million from Littlewoods with a 60p bet on a winning 8 from 10 Perm.

Most bets on the pools fall into the "harmless flutter" category, involving the outlay of small amounts of spare cash, yet offering the enticing prospect of a life-transforming win. And for most of the twentieth century, there was no cheaper or easier way for football fans to take a financial interest in the game they loved. Filling in the weekend pools coupon provides a direct stake in the outcome of every game played that weekend – not only those selected, which the punter hopes will end in a draw, but equally important, those *not* selected that you hope with equal fervour will end in an outright win for one side or another. A modest stake thus vests the announcement of the football results on a Saturday evening with great importance.

A Potted History of the Pools

The history of the modern pools dates back to the day in 1923 when John Moores and two partners set up a small office in Liverpool to offer gamblers the opportunity to bet on weekend football matches on coupons distributed to their clients during the week. The Moores operation – called Littlewoods after the aunt of one of the founding partners – was the first Pools firm to open for business. It was soon followed by Vernons in 1929, Zetters in 1933 and Empire Pools in 1935.

On the face of it, Pools betting represents a fair deal for the punter. Whereas fixed odds places the bookmaker in an adversarial relationship with the punter, the pools represented a reversion to the earlier concept of the bookmaker as a stakeholder responsible for administering the bets placed by different people, without any direct interest in the outcome.

Healthy competition between the four major players within the industry helped to ensure that the amount of the pool "taken off the top" to meet their administrative costs would be kept low, so most wagers placed would be returned to winning punters.

But the powers that be didn't quite see it that way. The 1933 *Report of the Royal Commission on Lotteries and Betting* recommended that all forms of off-course pool betting, including betting on football, should be prohibited.

To counter the threat posed by the Royal Commission's report, the pools operators formed an alliance with the Football Association and the Football League. The deal was that the operators would pay the FA and League a fee in return for using their fixtures on the coupons. In this way, some of the cash generated by gamblers was used for the benefit of the game itself, in a compromise which anticipated later arrangements for the National Lottery whereby gambling is acceptable provided some of the proceeds are given to "good causes".

During the Second World War, this idea was reinforced when the major pools companies amalgamated under the umbrella name of Unity Pools, and part of their proceeds were used to help finance the war effort. The post-war Labour Government decided to continue drawing on pools revenues to help finance public expenditure, and introduced a pools betting duty at 10% in early 1948. Later in the same year it was raised to 20%, and by 1961 it had increased to 33%. By the end of the 1980s, almost 50p in every £ wagered on the Pools was paid over to the government in duty. The 1990s saw some relaxation in the penal rates of duty, which was cut to 40% in 1990 and then 27.5% in 1994.

But even with these cuts, by the time the promoters, the football authorities, and the government have taken their cut, the amounts returned to the punters are pitifully small. During 1995, pools turnover was reported to be £723 million, of which just £172 million was returned to winners – or less than 25p of every £1 wagered.

Despite this, a report produced by Mintel in 1988, when pools duty was at its highest rate ever, reported that the pools was the most popular form of gambling in the UK. According to Mintel, more than a third of the adult population played the pools at some time during the year. Why?

5

Playing the Pools

The Treble Chance Pools

One of the major attractions of the pools over alternative forms of low stake / high return punting such as the National Lottery is that the outcome is not a matter of pure luck, but involves some application of skill and judgement. If anyone could accurately predict the results of individual matches, then they would stand to make substantial profits through the pools.

In reality, it is not quite as simple as this. To appreciate the size of the challenge, consider the following:

○ on average, approximately 30% of all football games played in the English Football League end in draws;
○ the fixed odds offered against draws by High Street bookmakers pricing up single games might typically be 9/4 against. Converting these odds into probabilities would imply that the gambler could earn a profit if he or she could identify which games would end in draws with a one-in-three accuracy or better;
○ so, assuming that some method could be devised to predict which games will end in draws with 35% accuracy, a gambler could beat the fixed odds game on single matches (ignoring for the moment the effects of betting tax);

○ but even with a 35% hit rate, the odds against correctly selecting any group of eight matches to end in draws would be more than 4,000 to 1. And remember, with the way the Pools operate, on the rare occasions you hit a winning line, you might have the misfortune to share the pot with a lot of other winning punters and get only a modest payout.

So, even if you could devise some system capable of forecasting which games would finish as draws with a high degree of accuracy, the odds would still be massively against you to scoop the Pools. Far better options would be to either bet on single matches (if available) or to take odds of 100/1 against four draws. Your chance of selecting four consecutive draws with a 35% success rate on any single match would be 1.5%, or 67/1 against. If you took odds of 100/1 on the sequence, you would generate a profit of 50% on a large series of bets – more than enough to make a fortune and without waiting a lifetime for a winning line!

If you are still tempted by the lure of a once-in-a-lifetime win, the biggest single pot is in the 'Treble Chance' football pool, first introduced in 1946, and so called because of the three possible outcomes of a game – home win, away win or draw. Draws are further categorised as "score" and "no-score". Score draws are defined as drawn games in which goals are scored, such as 1–1, 2–2 and 3–3 results. No-score draws are games ending 0–0. Of the 30% of games ending in draws, approximately 10% are no-score draws and 20% are score draws.

The punter's objective is to identify eight score draws. Eight correctly forecast score draws give the top prize, termed the 1st Dividend. The pools operators also offer several additional smaller dividends. The dividend you receive depends upon points gained. Each category of match result is allocated points as follows:

- Score Draw: 3 points
- No Score Draw or Void match: 2 points
- Home Win or Away Win: 1 point.

How to play the Pools

To fill in a coupon, the punter marks an 'X' against predicted score draws. It is important to avoid cancelled matches among the selections, as they will be declared void and are worth only two points. Announcements about cancelled matches are made in newspapers and on television during the days preceding the fixture date. In the event that extremely bad weather leads to a large number of cancelled matches in any weekend, a "Pools Panel" sits to determine which games would have ended in Score Draws had they been played. The Panel's judgement determines the results of the cancelled games for the purposes of the pools coupon, although obviously not for the league itself.

The total number of Xs that can be placed in any one column is determined by the type of pools entry you wish to submit. In the Full Cover Permutation, the most popular kind of pools entry, the punter selects more than eight matches in a single column of the pools coupon. If any group of eight games ends in score draws, this group will gain a maximum possible 24 points and share in the final dividend payout with other 24-point lines. For example, if you select ten matches in a column, you are effectively submitting 45 separate lines of eight selections each, as there are 45 possible permutations within the ten selected games which could give eight score draws. As the size of the permutation increases, so too does the number of entries and the total cost of the bet. For example, 12 selections yield 495 possible permutations of eight score draws, 15 selections yield 6,435 perms and 20 no less than 125,970 possible lines of eight draws.

To complete a pools coupon, you make your score draw forecasts and place an 'X' in the entry boxes on the coupon to indicate the selections. You would also have to enter the total cost of your bet, equal to the cost per line multiplied by the number of lines entered. The coupon also includes details of your name, address and telephone number. If you do not want details of winnings to be publicised, you place an 'X' in the 'no publicity' box. You then send a copy of the entry to the Pools Company, and retain a copy coupon to check match results. The coupon includes a unique reference number to be quoted if you make a claim for a prize. The pools companies generally ask that players submit claims for a 24–point line if there are eleven or less score draws among the Saturday matches. There are various telephone services, including freephone help lines, to deal with punters' queries.

When checking the coupon against the match results announced on Saturday evening, a punter does not need to add together the points gained by all of his or her selections, but only the best eight, as this is the line most likely to generate a dividend. Only if the best line is a winner is it worth looking at any of the others. In general, you need to have selected at least six score draws to have any chance of a dividend. Full details of dividend payouts are available from around mid-day on the Wednesday following the matches and are published in newspapers and on Teletext.

Anyone selecting eight score draws would get 24 points and be guaranteed a win dividend. But the size of the dividend would depend on the value of the pool for that weekend and the number of other winners. This in turn would be related to the number of games played that ended in score draws. For example, on

August 26th 2000, a fairly typical Saturday early in the 2000/01 season, a total of 46 games were played in Pools matches in England and Scotland, of which nine ended in score draws and three in no-score draws, generating a "good" dividend forecast.

What you as a Pools player are hoping for is that you will select eight score draws on your coupon, that those will be the only games ending in score draws that weekend – and hopefully, that no-one else has chosen the same eight games! But the chances of this happening are remote in the extreme. On a random basis, the odds against selecting eight score draws if the chance of any single game ending in a score draw is one in five (20%) would be 400,000 to 1 against. So it can be appreciated that a gambler relying on chance alone would be a little like the mythical monkey banging on typewriter keys for all eternity and only allowed to stop when it had typed out a Shakespeare play. In theory, it would have to happen eventually; in practice, the chances are that the poor monkey would be dead long before it had managed to type even the first line of *Romeo and Juliet* – unless it happened to be very lucky indeed!

Conclusions

The Pools have been an innocent source of entertainment for generations of British football fans. A few lucky ones have won millions with modest stakes. But they have done so through luck rather than skill. Regarded as a serious speculative activity, the Pools are a waste of time and effort. The overall payback of about 25p in every £1 wagered implies that they are impossible to beat by the application of skill and judgement.

So, if it is impossible to beat the Pools by skill, what accounts for their enduring popularity? There are two main factors: their entertainment value and the chance, however remote, of a big win. But unfortunately for the Pools operators, there is now another way of getting a rush from the prospect of becoming an instant millionaire called the National Lottery. The Lottery's arrival in the mid-1990s dealt the Pools a severe blow. And the advent of spread betting and online gambling means that there are now much better ways for football addicts to get their hit from betting on football than the Pools.

These factors suggest that the Pools may be slowly dying. At the very least, we can say with confidence that they will never regain the pre-eminent position in the world of football betting that they enjoyed for much of the twentieth century.

This may be no bad thing, because at the end of the day the pools are little more than a random game of chance that the intelligent speculator would be well advised to avoid.

6

Spread Betting, The Pools and Fixed Odds Compared

As the Pools slowly fade into history, serious football speculators are increasingly turning their attention to spread betting. As I have written a book entitled *Spread Betting to Win*, it will not surprise you to learn that I am far more enthusiastic about this form of gambling than about the Pools, or indeed about fixed odds betting.

To see why, let's compare the three forms of betting as methods of taking a position on individual games. I have selected ten criteria on which to make the comparison, awarding 3 points to the top-rated method, 2 to the second-rated and 1 to the third, giving a maximum possible total rating of 30 points for any method getting a top-rated 3 on all ten criteria.

Betting on the result

To my mind, a fundamental problem with Pools betting is that it requires the bettor to take simultaneous positions on a series of matches. If any of them are wrong, the entire bet loses. The spread firms price up individual games. So you can make a profit out of spread betting by selecting a few games of your choice, such as those involving just one team whose form you have analysed in depth. Fixed odds is somewhere between the two. Since 1990, it has been possible to bet on the outcome of single matches televised live, but for non-televised matches the standard rule remains minimum trebles. While it is clearly easier to pick three winning selections than eight, it is not as easy as targeting just one match.

Score on this criterion: Spread Betting 3; Fixed Odds 2; The Pools 1.

Cumulative score so far: Spread Betting 3; Fixed Odds 2; The Pools 1.

Betting "in running"

With the Pools, you make your selections some time before the game starts. On any game televised live, spread firms update their prices "in running", meaning you can place a wager at any time as a game proceeds. This gives an enormous advantage to anyone who can read the game. Some fixed odds firms do update their quotes in running on major games televised live, but they do this for fewer games than the spread firms, and also tend to close their books before the game ends.

Score: Spread Betting 3; Fixed Odds 2; The Pools 1.

Cumulative score so far: Spread Betting 6; Fixed Odds 4; The Pools 2.

Closing bets in running

With the Pools and Fixed Odds, once you have made a bet, you are locked into it until the final result is known. Fixed Odds is slightly superior to the Pools, in that you can "hedge" your bet by making another bet in the opposite direction, but this is far more cumbersome as a method of taking a profit than simply closing out a winning bet in running, as you can with the spread firms.

Score: Spread Betting 3; Fixed Odds 2; The Pools 1.

Cumulative score so far: Spread Betting 9; Fixed Odds 6; The Pools 3.

Betting on the size of the discrepancy

With spread betting, the gambler's profit or loss is not fixed, but varies directly with the extent of the deviation of the actual result from the gambler's predicted result. For example, in the England v. Germany game in Euro 2000, the amount you would have stood to win betting on England at fixed odds would have been the same no matter what the actual margin of victory. Conversely, a gambler who "bought" England on an index would have stood to win more, the greater England's margin of victory. I believe that this is to the advantage of an informed speculator, because the amounts won or lost provide a more accurate reflection of his or her judgement than a simple win-lose fixed-odds bet. It also means that you maintain interest in the game right up to the final whistle, which would not be the case in any game where one side was coasting to victory.

Score: Spread Betting 3; Fixed Odds and The Pools 1.

Cumulative score so far: Spread Betting 12; Fixed Odds 7; The Pools 4.

Risk exposure

A major advantage of both the Pools and Fixed Odds is that you know exactly how much you stand to lose at the time you make your bet. Your liability is equal to the value of the bet you make. With a spread bet, you do not know your potential exposure precisely in advance. While it is true that some spread firms, such as Hill Index, set upper limits to the loss that a client can suffer – normally five goals or 50 points – overall, spread betting compares unfavourably on this criterion, and so effective risk management is one of the most important requirements for successful spread betting.

Score: Fixed Odds and The Pools 3; Spread Betting 1.

Cumulative score so far: Spread Betting 13; Fixed Odds 10; The Pools 7.

Tax efficiency

Any gambler who plays the Pools pays a hefty duty to Her Majesty's Treasury for the privilege. And if you place a Fixed Odds wager through a high street bookmaker in Great Britain, you have to pay betting tax, either on the initial stake or on the amount won. It is possible to reduce your liability to betting tax, or even avoid it altogether, by betting offshore with bookies in the Channel Islands, over the Internet or betting at racecourses. But each of these methods involves time and effort to set up, and in the case of Internet betting, there is a further worry of not having a direct personal link to the bookie. By contrast, a gambler who places a wager with a spread firm does not have to pay tax on his or her winnings, as the tax charge is absorbed within the quoted spread. This means that spread

betting is the most tax-efficient form of off-course wager currently on offer in the United Kingdom.
Score: Spread Betting 3; Fixed Odds 2; The Pools 1.
Cumulative score so far: Spread Betting 16; Fixed Odds 12; The Pools 8.

Convenience

All spread bets are placed by phone, and subsequently verified in writing when the spread bookmaker sends a contract note to the client. Spread bets are therefore very easy to place. The gambler does not have to travel long distances on cold winter mornings to remote racecourses, or even go out in the rain to the nearest high street bookmaking shop. All that you need is a telephone at your side as you watch a football game live on television, together with your client reference number and the spread firm's telephone number.

For Fixed Odds betting, many bookmakers also offer their clientele the facility of credit accounts and telephone betting, but you cannot generally bet in running. More common methods of placing Fixed Odds bets are over the counter on the High Street or by travelling to a racecourse. The punter also has to return to the shop where the bet was placed in order to be paid, rather than getting a cheque through the post which is the standard settlement method for a spread bet.

With Pools betting, although it is fairly easy to complete and submit a Pools Coupon, checking the results afterwards can be complicated if you have selected a wide range of permutations.
Score: Spread Betting 3; The Pools 2; Fixed Odds 1.
Cumulative score so far: Spread Betting 19; Fixed Odds 13; The Pools 10.

Maximum payouts on winning bets

The big attraction of the Pools is that it offers the enticing prospect of a life-changing win for a small stake. Accumulator bets placed at Fixed Odds also offer potentially huge payouts if they win. For spread bets, the leverage is less – to win big, you must bet big, which obviously also exposes you to big losses should things turn sour.

Score: The Pools 3; Fixed Odds 2; Spread Betting 1.

Cumulative score so far: Spread Betting 20; Fixed Odds 15; The Pools 13.

Average return per bet

While there will be some winners among the gambling population, on average gamblers will lose money. If this weren't the case, bookmakers would not be in business. Not only do the bookmakers themselves have to make a return, but on top of that the government wants its share in taxes and duties, and in the case of the Pools, money is also paid to the FA and Football League for using their fixtures on the coupons.

Overall, the combined effect of these deductions means that the Pools returns less than 25p in the £ to the punters – a penal takeout of approximately three-quarters of all the money bet. The Fixed Odds bookmakers typically seek a return of 10–15%, in addition to which the government currently takes levies in betting duty, implying that about 75p-80p in the £ is returned to punters. Because of the lower overheads and superior tax efficiency of spread betting, the return here is approximately 85p-90p in the £.

Score: Spread Betting 3; Fixed Odds 2; The Pools 1.

Cumulative score so far: Spread Betting 23; Fixed Odds 17; The Pools 14.

The range of markets

The Pools offers the most restrictive choice of bets, with the punter only able to bet on the final result of the game. Fixed Odds bookmakers, under pressure from the spread firms, are becoming more imaginative in the range of prices they offer. But they still lag well behind the spread firms, who quote prices, not just on the final outcome, but on a whole raft of events that might happen during the game – the number of goals scored, bookings, corners, the performance of individual players, etc.

Score: Spread Betting 3; Fixed Odds 2; The Pools 1.
Cumulative score: Spread Betting 26; Fixed Odds 19; The Pools 15.

Summing Up

So pulling all these factors together, how do the three types of gambling compare?

Overall, spread betting scores best on most criteria. On my ratings, spread betting wins 26 points against 19 for Fixed Odds and 15 for the Pools. Fixed Odds betting has its place where you are looking to minimise your downside risks and have a clear view on which way a game may go, but are not sure of the likely margin of victory. To my mind, the Pools is strictly in the "harmless flutter" category: possibly OK for an occasional small bet to liven up the weekend, but emphatically not the way to make steady money from football. If you are serious about making money from football, there is only one way to go, and that is spread betting.

7

Euro96 and the Art of Arbitrage

Arbitrage Defined

The Oxford English Dictionary defines "arbitrage" as "traffic in bills of exchange or stocks to take advantage of different prices in other markets." The definition in Longmans' English Larousse is equally narrow. Arbitrage, it writes, is "the buying of goods in one place in order so to sell them immediately in another at a higher price; the buying of bills of exchange or stocks and shares for the same purpose."

As defined by these two sources, arbitrage is a risk-free exercise, which involves exploiting differences in prices between different markets to generate guaranteed profits.

Nice work if you can get it! This is not to say that opportunities for arbitrage of this type never arise in football betting. For example, if Sporting Index offered a spread of 2.2–2.4 on its Total Goals index for a particular game, while IG quoted 2.6–2.8 on the same match, you could arbitrage the two prices by *buying* Total Goals at 2.4 with Sporting while simultaneously *selling* at 2.6 with IG.

Unfortunately, because spread firms are not philanthropic institutions, such opportunities arise very infrequently. When they do, they are quickly eliminated by the activities of arbitrageurs.

But more subtle opportunities sometimes arise to exploit mispricings, not on the same market, but between different markets quoted on the same event.

For my definition of arbitrage is wider than that of the Oxford English Dictionary or Longmans' English Larousse. I would define arbitrage as follows:

Arbitrage involves taking two different positions on the same event or series of events such that overall risk exposure is reduced, as movements in one position are likely to be offset partly or wholly by countervailing movements in the other.

An example of this type of arbitrage occurred in the tournament indices quoted in Euro96.

Arbitraging Euro96: The Set-up

A major disadvantage of spread betting is that the speculator's maximum liability is not defined in advance. If you place a fixed odds bet of £100 on the outcome of a football match, you know that the most you can lose is £100. If you bet £100 a goal on the margin of supremacy of one team over another, your maximum liability could potentially run into several hundred pounds if you get things badly wrong.

A key requirement of successful spread betting is therefore to manage your risk, by setting a limit to the maximum exposure on any single event. The simplest way of doing this is by establishing a "stop-loss" limit when the bet is placed. But this costs money, and also implies a "stop-win" limit on the other side of the bet.

An alternative method is to arbitrage an event, by betting on different markets to reduce your overall exposure, as I did in Euro96.

At the beginning of Euro96, the generally available price about the total number of goals to be scored in the 31 tournament matches was 72–74, excluding Extra Time. So the index firms thought that, on average, approximately 2.35 goals per game would be scored during the 90 minutes of ordinary play.

Among the many other indices constructed for the tournament, City Index quoted a line of 310–330 seconds for the time of the fastest goal.

Examining these lines, it occurred to me that they appeared to be inconsistent with each other. If you forecast that 73 goals will be scored within a timeframe of 90 minutes, then logically the expected time of the first goal must be 90/73, or after 1.23 minutes or 74 seconds, assuming a random distribution.

But I then reflected on that final crucial point: *assuming a random distribution*.

Are goals randomly distributed through time in a football game?

Checking a sample of the time and number of goals scored in a sample of 500 games in the English and Scottish leagues, I discovered that they are not. In the sample I analysed, it turned out that about 40% of the goals were scored in the first half, and 60% in the second half. I can think of three possible reasons for this discontinuity:

○ *tactical changes*: at half-time, the coach has a chance to alter his team's tactics and formation in the light of his assessment of potential weaknesses in the opposition. An example was the changes made by Terry Venables during the half-time interval in the England-Scotland game played in Euro96. The 0–0 deadlock was broken early in the second half;
○ *changes in the context of the game*: at 0–0, both teams may

be as concerned not to concede a goal as they are to score one. Once a goal has been scored, the game tends to open up. At least one side – the team that is losing – needs to score a goal and so is forced to attack. The initial 0–0 equilibrium is more likely to have been disrupted in the second half than in the first half, so the second half of any game is likely to be more open than the early phases of the first half;

○ *physical tiredness* among players makes it more likely that mistakes will occur as the game progresses.

But although there is a clear discontinuity at half-time, a second conclusion of my analysis was that *within each half, goals appear to be randomly distributed through time.*

So if, in the course of Euro96, you anticipated that approximately 73 goals would be scored, you would expect that about 29 of these goals (40%) would be scored in the first half, and 44 in the second half. The statistical expectation before the tournament began would be for the first half goals to be spread over intervals of 1.55 minutes each (= 45/29).

In any small number of games such as the 31 to be played in Euro96, the distribution of goals actually scored would not precisely follow this pattern, but would be randomly distributed around it. But even allowing for a random distribution, City's opening quote of 310–330 seconds for the fastest goal looked way too high. On my analysis, it appeared unlikely that the fastest goal would take any longer than (2×95) or 180 seconds to score, *unless* far fewer than 73 goals were scored in the entire tournament.

To cover against this eventuality, I decided to set up an arbitrage position, by selling the total number of goals to be scored in the tournament at 72 while simultaneously selling the time of the fastest goal at 310 seconds.

Ideally, an arbitrageur aims for a similar profit whatever the outcome. In this case, I wanted the best chance of a profit and was indifferent as to whether it was generated by low (slow) scoring or high (fast) scoring. The hedge was established in the ratio of seconds to total goals, at 310/72 or about 4.5. I sold the time of the fastest goal for £10 per second while simultaneously selling total tournament goals with another spread firm at £45 per goal.

Arbitraging Euro96: The Denouement

In the event, the opening line for total goals quoted by the spread firms proved to be too high. A total of 63 goals were scored during normal time in Euro96, or just over 2 goals per game. This was one of the lowest recorded scoring rates in any major soccer tournament, so it is not surprising that the bookies got it slightly wrong.

The distribution of goals by phase of the tournament is shown in Figure 7.1. The graph divides the tournament into four phases: the eight games played in each of the three group qualifying rounds, followed by the seven games played in the quarter-finals, semi-finals and final. It shows that the number of goals scored per game increased through each successive qualifying round, from 13 in the first eight games to 25 in the last eight games of the qualifiers. The number of goals scored then fell back to only 8 in the seven games played in the final knockout stage of the tournament, a rate of barely more than one per game.

Figure 7.1
Total goals scored in each phase

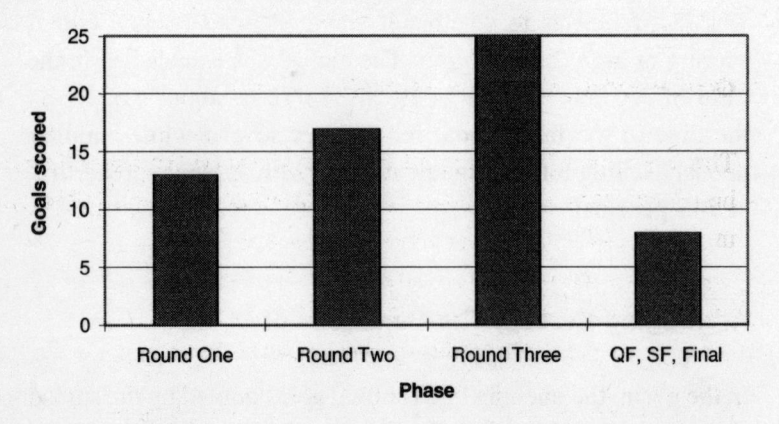

[Bar chart showing goals scored by phase: Round One ≈13, Round Two ≈17, Round Three =25, QF, SF, Final ≈8]

The low total of 63 goals scored in the tournament meant that the "sell" bet of £45 per goal at 72 goals yielded profits of (£45 × 9) or £405.

But the big profits came from the "fastest goal" line. The fastest goal in the tournament was Alan Shearer's scored in the semi-final between England and Germany after 132 seconds. By this time, the fastest goal bet was already comfortably in profit: in the qualifying rounds of the tournament, Stoichkov had scored for Bulgaria after 148 seconds in their game against Romania. The Shearer goal added to the profits, and meant that selling the time of the fastest goal for £10 per second at 310 seconds yielded a total return of (310–132) × £10, or £1,780.

The combined profit on the two positions was therefore £2,185.

The cynical may argue that this was just a lucky fluke. I would challenge such a conclusion. The profit was generated by a rational application of probability theory and statistical analysis to achieve an overwhelming likelihood of a positive return by exploiting inconsistencies in the different lines offered by the spread betting firms.

Goal scoring Times in Euro96

This conclusion is supported by an analysis of the time distribution of total goals scored in the tournament, which is given in Figure 7.2.

Figure 7.2
Times of goals scored

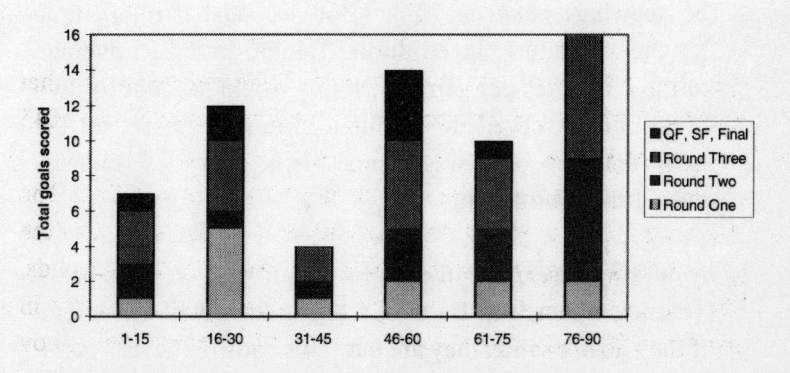

In Figure 7.2, the games played in Euro96 have been divided into six periods of 15 minutes each. The Figure shows that an average of 10.5 goals were scored in each 15-minute phase during Euro96. The incidence of goals was more or less randomly distributed through each half and each 15-minute phase. 37% of all goals were scored in the first half, and 63% in the second half – very similar to the 40:60 split in my sample of 500 English and Scottish league games. Only two periods are outside one standard deviation of the average of 10.5 goals per quarter-hour phase. The final 15 minutes of the first half appear to have been unusually quiet, while the greatest number of goals were scored in the final 15 minutes of the second half.

I believe that there are a couple of good reasons to suppose that the final quarter-hour of the game may be higher scoring than any other 15-minute phase in tournaments such as Euro96:

1. *The 90th minute is the longest minute in the game!* Because of injury time, the duration of this final phase is likely to be longer than the official duration 15 minutes. This is why so many goals are recorded as being scored in the 90th minute. The 90th minute is not 60 seconds at all, but can be anywhere between 90 and 360 seconds! If injury time for the 31 games played during Euro96 lasted an average of three minutes per game, then this would account for two of the goals scored in the final 15-minute phase, on the basis that one goal was scored about every 1.5 minutes during the tournament.

2. *Now or Never!* In the latter qualifying rounds of a Tournament such as Euro96, a losing team will know that, if they do not score, they are out. This "now or never" factor may extend to teams that are drawing or even winning, but not by enough to progress to the next round. Funnily enough, this does not apply in the same way to games in the knockout stages from the Quarter-Finals through to the Finals. Once through to these stages, teams still have the chance of 30 minutes of extra time and a penalty shoot-out, so if they are drawing going into the final quarter-hour of these games, they may be more concerned to defend than to attack. It is noteworthy that no goals at all were scored in the final 15 minutes of normal time in the knockout phase of Euro96.

In a correspondence on these issues in the columns of the monthly SMARTSig magazine, Torsten Lundgren wondered whether there was any evidence of a "90th minute" effect at the end of the first half as well. In Torsten's analysis, more goals might be scored in the 45th minute, because, like the 90th, it would be longer than sixty seconds because of first-half injury time. This may be the case, but I did not discover a higher than average scoring time in minute 45, at least in Euro96 – perhaps because the "now or never" factor does not apply at the end of the first half.

Torsten also argued that there was a lower than average chance of a goal being scored in the first or forty-sixth minute than during any other minute, because of the seconds it would take to set up the first attacking position from kick-off during each half.

This may help to account for City's high opening quote on the Time of the First Goals scored in the tournament. If, as Torsten Lundgren hypothesised, it is highly unlikely that a goal will be scored in the first 60 seconds of any game, then the City line of 310–330 seconds would effectively equate to a line of 250–280. Even so, it was still too high.

A second possible reason why City may have pitched their opening quote at such a high level relates to the asymmetric risk/return profile between selling and buying:

○ if I *sell*, then my maximum effective profit, assuming no goal will be scored in the first 60 seconds, would be (250 × unit stake). My maximum loss could be much more, if no goal was scored say in the first seven or eight minutes of any game in the competition. This was a distinct possibility, which is why I heaved a large sigh of relief when Stoichkov scored after 148 seconds in the Bulgaria v. Romania game;

○ on the other hand, if I *buy*, I know that my maximum loss is limited to (250 × unit stake), while the maximum profit could be many times more.

Most gamblers prefer to set a floor to their maximum loss, but no ceiling to their maximum gain. They also prefer a low chance of a large gain to a high chance of a small gain. So the spread firms know that there may be more buyers than sellers if the line is set at its true expected value. Therefore they may set the opening line slightly too high deliberately. Incidentally, this applies not just to football but to other sports such as cricket, where the Batsmen's Runs and Total Runs indices may be set slightly above statistical expectation to attract an equal number of buyers and sellers.

Conclusions

There was nothing particularly unusual about the goal distribution in Euro96. The number of goals scored in the first 15 minutes was slightly below average – 7 compared to an average of 10.5 per quarter hour – yet two goals were scored within the first 150 seconds and the fastest goal was scored after just 132 seconds. This was very close indeed to the mathematically expected time of the first goal. Given that seven goals were scored in the opening quarter-hour, you would expect the fastest goal to be scored after 15/7 minutes, or after 130 seconds: only 2 seconds different from the time of 132 seconds actually recorded.

It is remarkable what insights can be derived about a whole range of variables if soccer is analysed, not as a series of unconnected events, but rather as a mathematical system played within a finite universe bounded by time and space. As the Marquis de Laplace once observed, *"the most important questions of life are, for the most part, really only problems of probability."*

8

Goals Galore: World Cup, France '98

To be honest, I slightly shot myself in the foot in publishing my Euro96 coup in SMARTSig and later in *Spread Betting to Win*. When Euro 2000 came around, the pre-tournament lines on Total Goals and Time of the Fastest Goal were pretty much in line, so there was no opportunity to repeat the Euro96 arbitrage. I suspect that had I kept quiet things might have been different.

Nor were there any other obvious opportunities for arbitrage. One I looked at was whether there might be any opportunities to cross-trade the Total Goals quote for each team in the competition, and Total Goal Minutes. But the pre-tournament relationship between the two lines was almost perfect, as shown in Figure 8.1.

The horizontal axis shows the midpoint of pre-tournament quotes for the total number of goals scored by each of the sixteen nations in the competition, while the vertical axis shows the midpoint for total goal minutes. The trendline shows an almost perfect relationship between them. The higher the number of goals, the greater the total goal minutes. It is clear from the figure that IG expected Spain, Holland, France and Italy to make it through to the semi-finals – prescient forecasts, as it turned out – and, because they would go furthest, they would score most goals and tot up most goal minutes.

Figure 8.1
The relationship between Total Goals and Total Goal Minutes quotes in Euro 2000

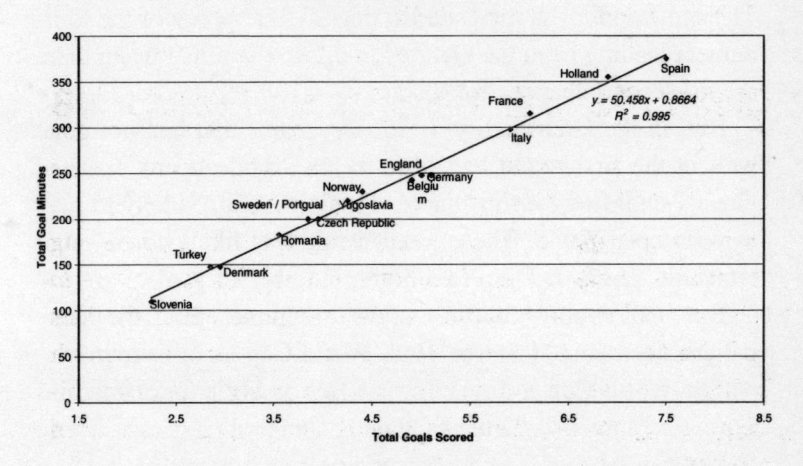

[Scatter plot showing data points for: Slovenia, Turkey, Denmark, Sweden/Portugal, Norway, Romania, Czech Republic, Yugoslavia, England, Germany, Belgium, Italy, France, Holland, Spain. Trend line: $y = 50.458x + 0.8664$, $R^2 = 0.995$. X-axis: Total Goals Scored (1.5 to 8.5). Y-axis: Total Goal Minutes (0 to 400).]

Source: IG Index, pre-tournament quotes

Had the two quotes been out of line for any single team, then there might have been the opportunity to arbitrage them. For example, if a particular team had been given a high Total Goals quote and a low Goals Minutes quote, you could have bought goal minutes and sold total goals and made money whatever happened.

Sadly, no such obvious arbitrage opportunities were evident in the pre-tournament prices. But my research on Euro96 had thrown up some other interesting findings that might have some application in Euro 2000.

I recalled the curious pattern of the number of goals scored in each round of the tournament: gradually increasing in the first three qualifying rounds, before falling back again in the knock-out stage. I suspected that this pattern might be explained by strategic considerations. In the opening qualifying round of a tournament such as Euro96, it was as important to avoid defeat as to achieve victory. The result was tight defensive matches. The same applies in the "sudden death" final phase of the tournament leading from the Quarter-Finals to the Final, when there are no second chances for losers.

But, in the later qualifying rounds, teams that had not done well in the first round had little to lose, while teams that had already qualified for the Quarter-Finals were also likely to play a more open game. The overall result was likely to be more attacking games leading to a higher number of goals.

But one swallow doesn't make a summer. Had the same pattern been evident in the 1998 World Cup as in Euro96?

The World Cup in France was twice as big a tournament as Euro96, comprising 32 teams playing a total of 64 games. These games can be analysed as comprising four phases, each of 16 games. The first three phases represent each of the three successive qualifying rounds. The final phase represents the final knock-out stage of the tournament played between the sixteen qualifiers.

At France '98, a total of 170 goals had been scored during normal playing time, or an average of just over 2.65 goals per game. As I analysed the goalscoring pattern at the World Cup, five general points emerged.

1. *The pattern of scoring was not normally distributed, but showed a slight positive skew*. This can be seen in Figure 8.2, which shows the distribution of total goals scored in the 64 games played in the 1998 World Cup.

Figure 8.2
Distribution of total goals scored in the 64 games played in France '98

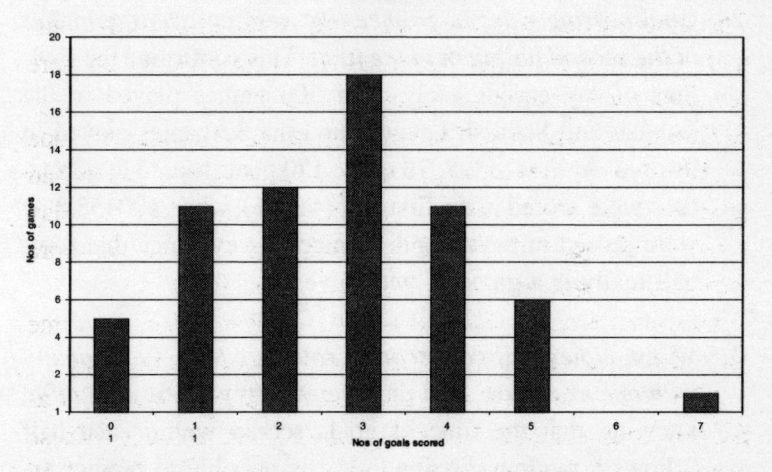

The Figure shows that five of the games ended in no-score draws, while in eleven a single goal was scored. Twelve games ended with two goals; 18 with three; 11 with four, 6 with five and in one game seven goals were scored. The average scoring rate was 2.65 goals per game, with a mode of 3 goals.

This pattern reinforces the point that it is slightly riskier to sell Total Goals than to buy them. A buyers' exposure is limited to the difference between the buying price, typically around 2.7, and zero. A sellers' exposure could be much greater than this in a high-scoring match. This is not to say that selling Total Goals in a game is always a bad idea, only that you need to be careful in sizing your unit bet in relation to total bankroll. Anyone selling aggressively into the Spain v. Bulgaria match, the highest scoring game at France '98 which ended in a 6–1 Spanish victory, would have suffered significant losses.

2. *Goal scoring rates at France '98 were on average higher in the second half than in the first.* This confirmed the findings of my earlier analysis of 500 games played in the English and Scottish Leagues and the 32 games played in Euro96. At France '98, 70 of the 170 goals scored in normal time were scored in the first half (41.2%), while 100 (58.8%) were scored in the second. Compelling evidence that football really *is* a game of two halves!

3. *Within either half goal scoring rates are broadly random – with one exception.* As I discovered to my profit in Euro96, knowing that the time of goals scored within each half follows a random distribution, it is possible to predict the likely time of the fastest goal scored in a Tournament with reasonable accuracy. It is equal to

45 minutes / (Total goals forecast × 40%)

So in the 1998 World Cup, the generally available opening price of 164–167 on the Total Tournament Goals spread implied that the index bookmakers expected around 165 goals to be scored in the entire Tournament – a pretty accurate forecast, as it turned out. Yet the spread firms opened their Time of Fastest Goal quote at 180–200 seconds. Like the opening Fastest Goal quote at Euro96, this was way too high in relation to the total goals forecast. Applying the formula, we find that the expected time of the fastest goal in the competition would have been

$$45 \text{ minutes} / (166 \times 40\%) = 45 \text{ minutes} / 66.4 =$$
$$0.68 \text{ minutes} = 41 \text{ seconds}$$

Of course, you would have been cautious about selling at much below 60 seconds, taking account of Torsten Lundgren's prudent observation that it is less likely that goals will be scored within a minute of kick-off in either half. But even so, selling at 180 seconds would have represented an excellent bet. The fastest goal scored in the 1998 World Cup came 52 seconds into the Nigeria v. Paraguay game. This is around 11 seconds slower than the time that would have been forecast by a simple application of the formula.

So in France '98, as in Euro96, it would have been possible to make a substantial low-risk profit by arbitraging the Total Goals and Time of Fastest Goal lines.

4. Although goalscoring rates are broadly randomly distributed in each half, *more Tournament goals are scored in the final 15 minutes of the game than in any of the preceding five 15-minute periods*. I am not sure if the same would apply to league games, but in tournaments such as the World Cup or European championship, this seems to be a general phenomenon, for the reasons analysed in the last chapter.

For the World Cup in 1998, the goalscoring pattern by 15-minute period, round by round, is shown in Figure 8.3.

On average, with 170 goals scored in the entire tournament, you would expect about 28 goals to have been scored in each of the six 15-minute intervals played between the first and 90th minute of the games. In fact, as Figure 8.3 shows, between 20 and 31 goals were scored in each of the first five 15-minute intervals, or an average of approximately 0.4 goals per period per game. *But no less than 43 goals were scored in the final 15 minutes of all 64 games played in the 1998 World Cup.*

This is the same phenomenon as was observed in Euro96. The final quarter-hour of the game seems to be much higher scoring than any other 15-minute period.

Figure 8.3
Total goals scored in each 15-minute period of the 1998 World Cup

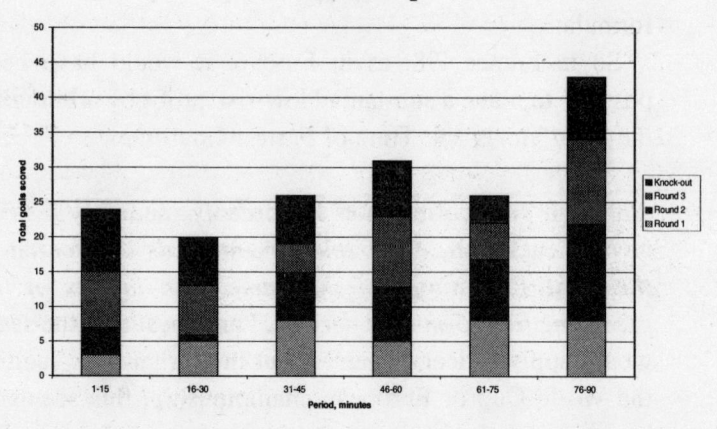

5. *Within successive rounds of football tournaments, the scoring rate is not constant, but tends to increase through each successive qualifying round, before falling back in the games played in the final knock-out stages.* This was evident in Euro96. In a news release issued by Oldcastle Books on June 13th 1998, after the first seven games of the 1998 World Cup, I predicted on the basis of this theorem

that goal scoring rates would accelerate through France '98 as well.

The release was as follows:

"A football tournament is like a poker tournament," says Jacques. "In the early rounds, tight defensive play may be the optimal strategy. At this stage, it is as important to avoid defeat as it is to achieve victory. But in the later rounds, you may be forced to adopt a more aggressive strategy to survive. Teams that have not done well in the first round have to go all out for a win if they are to have any chance of going through to the knock-out stages, while teams that have already qualified are also likely to play a more open game."

Jacques points to the evidence of Euro96 to support his views. As for the World Cup, the tournament began with three qualifying rounds. "In Round 1, there were less than 2 goals per game. In Round 2, average goals per game rose to over 2. And in Round 3, the average was more than 3 goals per game."

The implication could be that it is worth buying the Total Goals spread with one of the index firms. Their pre-tournament lines were typically 164–167, implying that they forecast around 2.6 goals per game. "Certainly I will be looking to buy if the spread drops to less than 160 goals during Round 1," Jacques stated.

The rate of acceleration in the World Cup was not as fast as in Euro96, but nevertheless was clearly in evidence, as can be seen in Figure 8.4.

Figure 8.4
Average goals scored per game in each phase of the 1998 World Cup

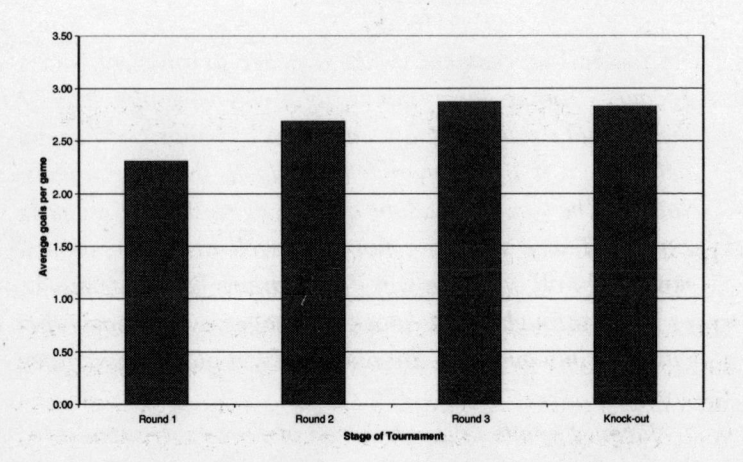

It was time to apply this analysis to Euro 2000.

9

Euro 2000: the knockout stages

The Set-up

The thesis that I had developed regarding goalscoring rates during football tournaments is far from being an iron law. But there does seem to be a general tendency for goalscoring rates to increase round-by-round in the qualifying phases of international tournaments before falling back in the knockout phase, as is shown in Figure 9.1

Figure 9.1
Goalscoring rates in international football tournaments

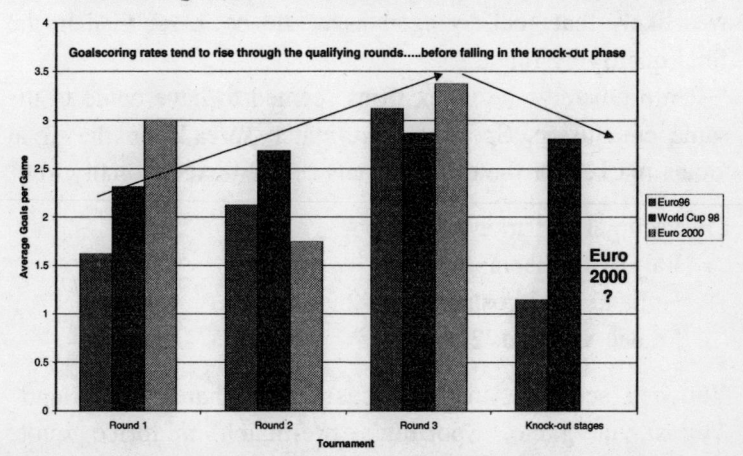

There are bound to be some exceptions to the general rule that goalscoring rates tend to increase through the successive qualifying rounds before falling back in the knockout phase. In fact, Euro 2000 had already witnessed such an exception. The average goalscoring rate in the second qualifying round had been just 1.75 goals, significantly lower than in the first round, as can be seen in Figure 9.1. Nevertheless, there seem to be sound strategic reasons for supposing that teams are likely to play more open, attacking football in the final qualifying round of a tournament, either in a last ditch attempt to get through, or because, for teams that have already qualified, the result does not matter a great deal. Such teams may revert to something close to the old Corinthian principle – that it doesn't matter whether you win or lose, only how you play the game – and seek to experiment and entertain. But once teams enter into sudden death contests in the quarter and semi-finals, things become deadly serious once more and they are likely to be concerned above all not to concede any soft early goals.

So as I considered the pre-match prices going into the quarter-finals of Euro 2000, I was convinced in my own mind that it was likely that goalscoring rates would be lower than in the final qualifying round.

Unfortunately, the index firms seemed to have come to the same conclusion. Sporting's pre-match spreads on the Total Goals market for the quarter-finals seemed exceptionally low:

- Portugal v. Turkey: 2.3–2.6
- Italy v. Romania: 2.2–2.5
- Holland v. Yugoslavia: 2.6–2.9
- France v. Spain: 2.3–2.6.

You can see that, in every case other than the Holland–Yugoslavia game, Sporting's pre-match midprice quote anticipated that less than 2.5 goals would be scored on average in each game.

These prices were far from generous for someone looking to sell the Total Goals line. By shopping around among the other spread firms, I was able to get a slightly better price on some of the games, but in the end was only able to sell the Total Goals lines for £100 per goal at the following prices:

- Portugal v. Turkey at 2.4
- Italy v. Romania at 2.3
- Holland v. Yugoslavia at 2.7
- France v. Spain at 2.4.

Despite the tight pricing on Total Goals, as I sat back to enjoy the quarter-finals on Saturday June 24th, all seemed set fair for a pleasant weekend's entertainment, which, I confidently expected, would prove further evidence of my Tournament Goals hypothesis, and generate a modest profit on my £100 per goal stake.

Little did I realise then that the weekend would have a particularly vicious sting in its tail.

The Quarter-Finals

The weekend of the Euro 2000 quarter-finals started well enough. On Saturday afternoon in Brussels, Italy scored two first half goals against Romania, before settling back and letting the East Europeans chase the game in the second half. The highly disciplined Italian defence absorbed the pressure without too much difficulty, and the final 2–0 result yielded a modest £30 profit at the final whistle.

It was a similar story in the Portugal-Turkey game. A couple of goals by Nuno Gomez either side of half-time saw the Portuguese run out as 2–0 winners, worth a further £40 to me.

Sadly, most of these profits were given back the following day when three goals were scored in the France-Spain game, resulting in a net loss of £60 on my "sell" position. But I was still reasonably sanguine as Holland v. Yugoslavia kicked off on Sunday evening. My equanimity was barely disturbed by a spectacular one-two in the 23rd minute, when Bergkamp received a pass from Kluivert and deftly chipped the ball back over a flat defence for Kluivert to run onto and score. Even when, a few minutes before half-time, Edgar Davids curled a pass onto Kluivert's right foot for him to make it 2–0, my peace of mind was barely disturbed. At half-time, I felt that the game was looking a bit like the previous day's clash between Italy and Romania, and perhaps Holland would be content to defend their lead in second half and let Romania chase the game.

Holland v. Yugoslavia: the Second Half

How wrong can you be? Five minutes into the second half, Bosvelt dribbled his way past an opponent and sent in a low cross that Kluivert duly converted. Three minutes later, Holland's star striker got his fourth, when Numan chipped to Zenden, who dribbled past a Yugoslav defender before laying it back to Kluivert.

On the field the football was sublime, and Holland were producing the finest attacking display of the tournament. But funnily enough I was not enjoying this master class as much as perhaps I should have been. Even when Kluivert was substituted, there was little respite. In the 77th minute, Bergkamp placed a cross to Mark Overmars, who insouciantly flicked the ball up and volleyed it into the top corner. Overmars scored again towards the end, but just as I was nursing my wounds and calculating the damage that a 6–0 Dutch victory would do to my bankroll, there was a final *coup de grace*. A last-ditch effort from a Yugoslav striker hit the crossbar; the ball rebounded; and Savo Milosevic banged in a consolation goal for Yugoslavia.

Figure 9.2
A Seller's Nightmare: The Total Goals Index,
Holland v. Yugoslavia

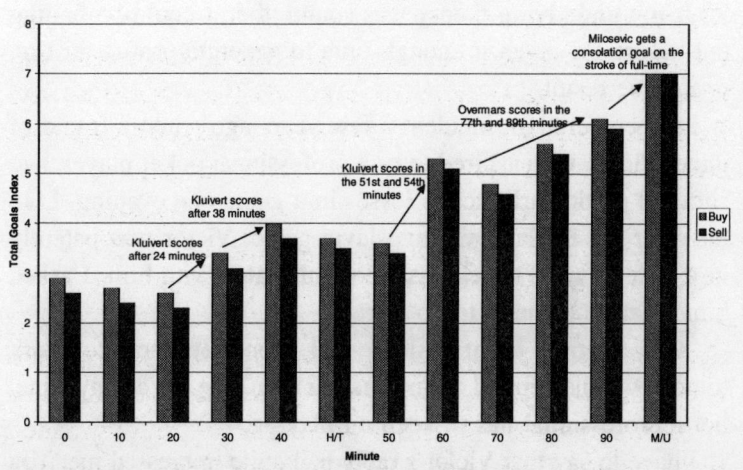

Source: Sporting Index quotes in running during the game, June 25th 2000

Overall, it had been a great night for the Dutch, a bad night for the Yugoslavs, and a truly dreadful night for me. The seven-goal soccerfest had cost me £430 and severely dented my confidence in my own goalscoring theory.

The closing stages

I was still reeling from the shock of Sunday night when the semi-finals came round in midweek. To be honest, at that point I was wondering whether the best thing to do might just be to gracefully withdraw from battle and accept defeat on the Total Goals line.

But the worry at the back of my mind was how I would feel if the last three matches were all low scoring. What if the Holland v. Yugoslavia match had simply been an outlier, one of those rare exceptions that tests a rule but does not disprove it? If my underlying theory was sound, then I could be bailing out before I'd given it enough time to generate profits, just on one rogue result.

I remembered an incident a few years ago when a friend of mine, Victor, who aspired to be a professional poker player, had suffered particularly heavy losses in a game one evening. Like me after the Holland v. Yugoslavia game, Victor was patently in a state of mild shock. As I commiserated with him, I asked him what he planned to do next.

"Get a good night's sleep and then get back to work tomorrow," he replied. "An amateur can give up at any time; but a professional has to keep on playing."

I have to say that Victor's reply had quite impressed me. You will have gathered by now that, at the bet levels at which I play, with a basic bet of £100 and a maximum exposure of £500 per bet, I do not aspire to make a living out of betting on football. At the same time, these bets represent more than a fun flutter. Although £500 is not enough to make any significant difference to my lifestyle, it is enough to be able to buy some little luxury to reward myself when things are going well – or to force me to cut back for a couple of weeks if things are running against me.

And I do take my speculative activities seriously, playing to win, whether on the card table, in sports betting or on the financial markets. Quite apart from the money involved, there's the little matter of self-respect. I only play in contests involving some degree of skill, and would like to regard myself as a skilful player. The sums won or lost are an unambiguous measure of skill.

To meekly accept defeat and retire from the fray after one £430 hit went against the grain.

So I decided to continue selling the Total Goals index into the semi-finals and finals of Euro 2000. Only if I suffered another couple of heavy losses would I abandon the Total Goals system completely.

And I'm happy to report that, in the closing stages of Euro 2000, my luck *did* change.

It changed partly because the lines themselves were slightly higher in the semi-finals and finals. Clearly I had not been the only seller of Total Goals in the quarter-finals, nor the only person to be hammered by the 6–1 Dutch victory. The spread firms seemed to have adjusted their lines upwards to take account of the carnage among sellers.

You often find this in gambling. Following an exceptional swing in one direction, the line on the next game is adjusted in that direction. It makes sense. The winners on the previous game are likely to be playing up their winnings with heavier bets, while the losers will be the state of retreat, operating off smaller bankrolls, maybe forced to cut their bets or drop out of the market altogether. Such situations can present viable betting opportunities, because through time the actual run of results is likely to revert back the historic average.

That, at least, was what I hoped as I nervously placed two Sell orders, both at 2.6, on Total Goals in the Portugal v. France and Italy v. Holland semi-finals of Euro 2000.

But on the night of the games I didn't feel inclined to watch them, and went out to the cinema instead.

Only on return did I learn that both games had ended in draws, and been finally decided in extra time. On Wednesday night, the 1–1 deadlock between Portugal and France was broken by a penalty awarded to the French in extra time. The Thursday game between Holland and Italy ended goalless, and the game was finally decided in Italy's favour by a penalty shoot-out.

So the two semi-finals generated total profits of £320 for me; not quite enough to eliminate the losses sustained on the Holland v. Yugoslavia match, but enough to persuade me to persevere into the final.

But the best price I could secure on Total Goals in the France v. Italy game was 2.3–2.6. Selling at 2.3, it looked like I was finally going to grind ahead as Italy stoutly defended a 1–0 lead right into the closing seconds. But there was a final twist in this most dramatic of international tournaments. A rare aberration caught the Italian defence napping almost on the closing whistle and let in Wiltord for the French equaliser. The French duly went on to take the title against the demoralised Italians with a golden goal in extra time.

So where does all this leave my Total Goals system? Overall, I lost £70 selling Total Goals in the knockout stages of Euro 2000. If the Holland v. Yugoslavia match was excluded, then overall I would have made a £350 profit. But that of course is the point. In real life, speculating with real money, you cannot dismiss "unusual events". You have to pay for them and be ready to absorb the loss. As a seller, you have strictly limited upside but face unlimited downside risk. Every now and then, an unusually high scoring game is going to come along and hit you where it hurts.

Does this mean that the only viable alternative is on the Buy side? Not necessarily. Provided that, over time, Sell positions yield aggregate profits, then an intelligent speculator should be prepared to absorb the occasional big loss.

But, after the experience of Euro 2000, the jury is still out as to whether selling Total Goals in the knockout stages of an international football tournament is indeed a profitable play. Much depends on the best price that you can get for selling goals. Despite the catastrophe of the Holland v. Yugoslavia game, had I just been able to get an extra 0.1 point on the Sell price in each of the games, the sequence of bets would have washed its face.

My overall conclusion is that goalscoring rates are probably likely to be lower in the knockout phase than in the final qualifying round, but that selling Total Goals may only represent a viable system if you can secure an average price of 2.5 or better. And of course you have to be capable of absorbing the occasional big loss in a high scoring game!

10

Punting on football shares

Football Mania

Every so often, the Stock Market loses touch with reality. Supposedly rational investors become a trampling herd, rushing in to buy the latest craze, driving share prices way above any level that can be realistically justified by future profits and dividends.

The mob mentality that led to the Football Mania of the mid-1990s may not have quite been on a par with the seventeenth century Dutch Tulipomania, the English Railway Mania of the 1840s, or even the Dot.Com Bubble of the late 1990s. But in its way, the 1990s Football Mania represents another cautionary tale of Extraordinary Popular Delusions and the Madness of Crowds.

The British Football Revolution

Looking back, it seems remarkable that, as recently as 1990, the only football club quoted on the London stock exchange was Tottenham Hotspur. At the time, Spurs were regarded as an eccentric exception by football fans and investors alike. The conventional wisdom was that football clubs could not be regarded as conventional commercial enterprises suitable for listing on the Stock Market. Their principal "assets" were not property or plant and machinery, but people, in the shape of players and coaching staff. It seemed ethically wrong to treat them as mere balance sheet items. And in 1990 most Stock Market analysts would have argued that, even if you wanted to, it would be extremely difficult to ascribe reliable balance sheet values to players, because such values might be instantly destroyed by nothing more than a bad tackle.

Then there was revenue stream. The conventional way of pricing company shares is to discount the future expected stream of profits they will generate to arrive at a current valuation. In 1990, most analysts would have expressed the view that the revenue streams of football clubs could not be reliably forecast. Club revenues can fluctuate widely depending on factors such as promotion and relegation, cup runs, and, for the top clubs, success in European competition. And if a club had a run of success, fan pressure would force the Board to reinvest the proceeds in new players and facilities. There would be little if any left for shareholder dividends even when times were good.

For these reasons, the best kind of club owner from the fans' viewpoint were wealthy benefactors, such as the Moores family who reinvested some of their Littlewoods Pools fortune into Liverpool FC, Elton John at Watford or Jack Walker at Blackburn Rovers, who treated their clubs as expensive hobbies into which they were prepared to pump a steady stream of money in return for the pleasure that supporting the club gave them.

So, in the view of most financial analysts at the beginning of the 1990s, the most appropriate shareholders for a club were likely to be wealthy fans, who would treat their investment like an expensive Season Ticket.

This traditional view was turned upside down in the 1990s.

The Taylor Report commissioned after the Hillsborough disaster recommended significant improvements in stadium facilities to make sure that such a tragedy could never happen again. The key requirement of the Taylor Report was that old terraced stand areas should be replaced by all-seater stadia. This requirement implied a major investment programme for every club in the football league to upgrade and replace their existing stadium facilities.

The funding necessary to implement the programme was beyond the financial means of all but the wealthiest backers. Although clubs did benefit from grant assistance, many had to turn to external investors for additional support. The consequence was a flurry of listings in the early and mid-1990s, so that by October 1997, when Nottingham Forest floated as a publicly listed company, a total of 21 English and Scottish football clubs were listed on either the main stock market, the Alternative Investment Market (AIM) or the over-the-counter market (OFEX).

Stock Market listing radically altered the way in which football clubs were run. No longer could they operate purely as the pet hobbies of millionaire owners. Listing meant that they had to be properly managed as commercial entities submitting audited annual accounts and aiming to trade at a profit. External investors also pressed for a return on their shares in the form of a dividend. This often generated tension between the investors, concerned that their clubs should trade profitably and pay at least a nominal dividend, and the fans who believed that their football club should use any surpluses to improve the playing squad and facilities.

The rich get richer

The Deloitte and Touche *Annual Review of Football Finance* shows that, although the revenues of all English league clubs grew rapidly during the 1990s, the combined turnover of the twenty Premier League clubs grew significantly faster than that of the 72 clubs in the Nationwide Football League. The trends are shown graphically in Figure 10.1 below.

Figure 10.1
The rich get richer: Turnover in English professional football, 1993/94–2001/02

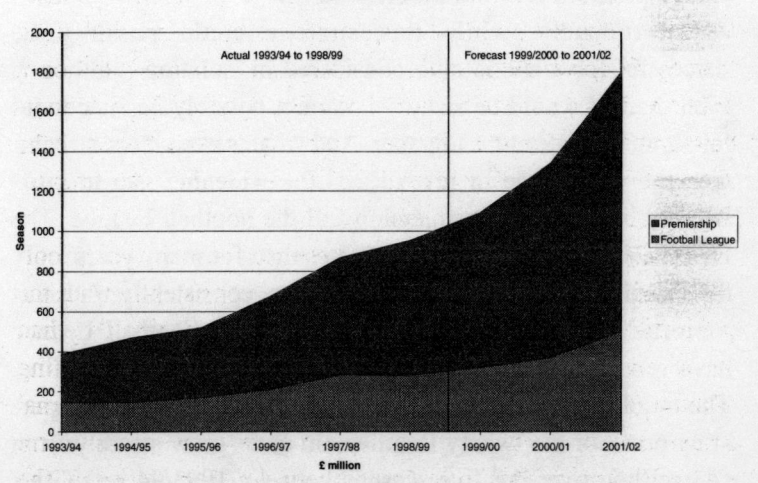

Source: Deloitte & Touche, *Annual Review of Football Finance*, August 2000, p.11

Figure 10.1 shows that, over the period between 1993/94 and 1998/99, Premiership revenues almost tripled, from £241 million to £670 million. The growth of Football League revenues was much less impressive, up from £145 million to £281 million.

Moreover, Deloitte & Touche forecast that the divergence between the Premiership and the rest of the league would widen even more over the next four years. The accountants commented that "in 2001/02, we estimate that the average income differential between a Premier League and Division One club will have grown to a massive £51.5 million." They concluded by asking, "How on earth does one close that gap?"

The answer given by a growing number of Nationwide Football League clubs is to try to buy their way to success, spending more on players than they are earning in income, and gambling that their operating losses will eventually be wiped out by promotion to the Premier tier.

Unfortunately, while this strategy could possibly be successful for a single club considered in isolation – although even there it would be risky – it cannot possibly be successful for all the League clubs together. And what is even more striking than the divergence in revenues is the widening gap in profitability between the Premiership and the Football League. The Deloitte and Touche Review indicates that, for many years, only the Premier league clubs as a group have consistently traded at a profit. The clubs in the three divisions of Football League have returned operating losses that have grown through time. The trend is shown in Figure 10.2, which reveals that the operating profit of the twenty Premiership clubs grew steadily from £41 million over the five seasons between 1993/94 and £95.8 million in 1997/98, before falling back to £68.8 million in 1998/99. But, over the same period, the combined operating loss of the 72 Football League clubs rose inexorably from £16 million in 1993/94 to £68.5 million in 1998/99, an average loss of almost £1 million per club per year.

This trend has set alarm bells ringing at Deloitte & Touche, who have consistently issued dire forecasts of bankruptcies and liquidations in the lower divisions unless action is taken to bring their player wages back into line with the levels that can be paid out of club revenues.

Figure 10.2
The operating profits of English League clubs, 1993/94–1998/99

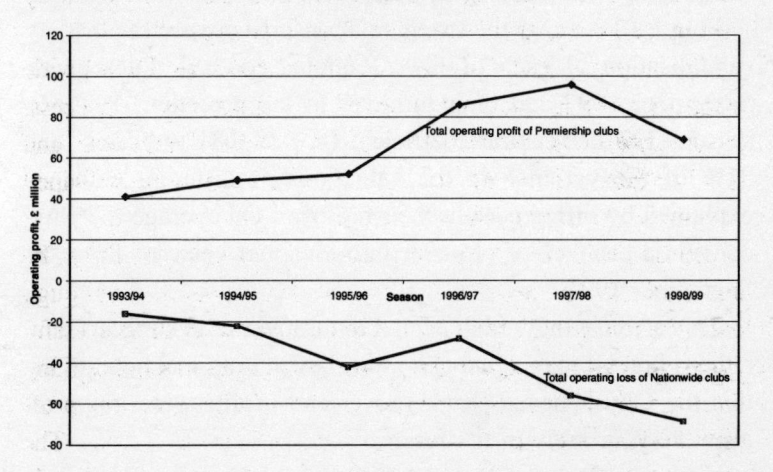

Source: Deloitte & Touche, *Annual Review of Football Finance*, August 2000, p.12

Despite the mounting losses of Football League clubs, forecasts of financial disaster have yet to be realised on a large scale. Whenever any club has run into financial difficulties, as for example in the case of Millwall or Crystal Palace in late 1990s, new investors have generally been willing to come in to the pick up the pieces and carry on much as before. On the face of it, such lemming-like behaviour would appear to be a classic case of throwing good money after bad.

So how can it be explained?

The valuation of quoted football clubs

In late 1997, I analysed the valuation of quoted football clubs, and discovered that the single most important determinant of market capitalisation was their turnover. The relationship is shown graphically in Figure 10.3 below.

Figure 10.3 shows the strong relationship between the market capitalisation of each of the 21 quoted football clubs as at September 1997 and their turnover in the preceding 1996/97 season. The correlation coefficient (R^2) of 0.81 indicates that 81% of the variance in the valuations of different clubs is explained by differences in their turnover. On average the City converted each £1 of turnover into a capital value of £7 as at September 1997.

This astonishingly high capital to turnover ratio suggests that either Football mania had gone well beyond rational bounds, or that the City believed that turnover and profits were going to grow very strongly in the future.

Figure 10.3 shows that the City valued Manchester United more highly than any other club in the English or Scottish leagues, reflecting United's significantly higher turnover. The next most highly valued clubs were the "chasing pack" of Newcastle, Chelsea and Arsenal and the dominant Scottish club, Rangers, followed by other leading English and Scottish clubs such as Leeds United, Spurs, Aston Villa and Celtic.

But there was quite a gap between Manchester United and the rest. While Manchester United had a market value of over £400 million in September 1997, the chasing pack were each valued at between £150 million and £200 million, and the other established Premiership clubs typically had market capitalisations around £100 million.

Figure 10.3
Market capitalisation and turnover of quoted British football clubs, September 1997

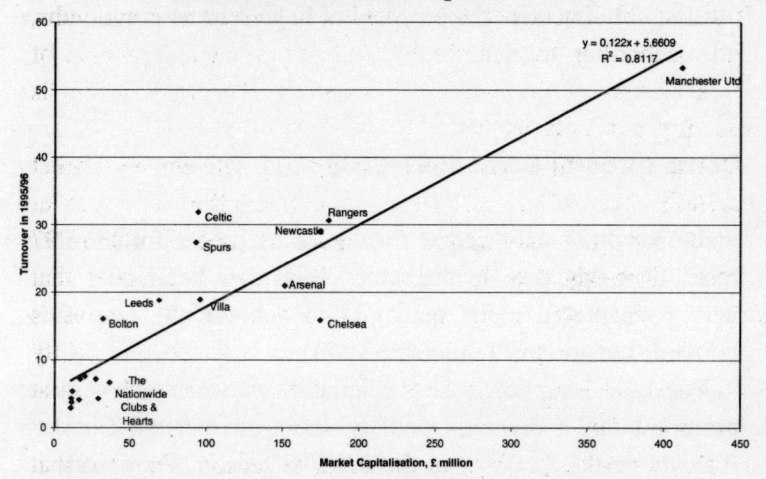

Chart showing turnover in 1995/96 (y-axis, 0-60) vs Market Capitalisation, £ million (x-axis, 0-450). Regression line: $y = 0.122x + 5.6609$, $R^2 = 0.8117$. Data points labelled: Manchester Utd, Celtic, Rangers, Newcastle, Spurs, Arsenal, Leeds, Villa, Bolton, Chelsea, The Nationwide Clubs & Hearts.

Source: Financial Times for market capitalisation, Deloitte & Touche *Annual Review of Football Finance*, 1998, for 1996/97 turnover figures

For clubs out of the Premiership, valuations slumped dramatically. The market capitalisation of clubs in the Football League typically ranged between £10 million and £30 million.

Somewhere between these two groups was Bolton Wanderers, at that time a Premiership club, but subsequently relegated. The City regards "yo yo" clubs such as Bolton who go up and down between the Premiership and Football Leagues as inferior investments, and discounts their values accordingly.

The yawning gap between the value of Premiership and Football League status provides a clue as to why wealthy individuals continue to be willing to pump money into clubs lower down the league. They may be loss makers paying wages well in excess of current revenues, but they offer a potential vehicle for buying in to the dream of Premier League status. They are akin to venture capital investments which come with a high risk of loss, but also offer the prospect of huge returns if everything goes according to plan.

Boom turns to Bust: 1997–2000

Sadly for those who nursed dreams of making a fortune from football in this way, in the three years after September 1997 very few quoted clubs managed to achieve the leap from Football League to Premiership status.

The one exception was Sunderland, who narrowly missed promotion in a dramatic penalty shoot-out against Charlton Athletic on the final day of the 1997/98 season. They made no mistake the following year. Sunderland then confounded many sceptics by doing exceptionally well in their first season in the Premiership in 1999/2000, when they were unlucky not to qualify for Europe. The City duly recognised their achievement, and by September 2000 Sunderland's market value was 20% higher than it had been three years previously, at £33 million.

At the other end of the scale, Sheffield United's valuation tumbled almost 80% from £29 million to £7 million as they proved unable to regain their Premiership status. Sheffield United were the biggest faller among the quoted football clubs, but elsewhere the overall picture was also gloomy. The hype that had greeted their initial public offerings had worn off by September 2000, and the City was once again applying fundamental investment criteria and found most clubs wanting.

Overall, the total capitalisation of the quoted clubs excluding Manchester Utd declined from £1,280 million to £970 million between September 1997 and September 2000. Almost without exception, quoted clubs outside the Premiership experienced sharp declines in their market value. The club-by-club picture for the quoted Premiership clubs and for Rangers and Celtic, the two leading Scottish clubs, is shown in Figure 10.4.

Figure 10.4
Market Capitalisation of the English and Scottish Premiership clubs

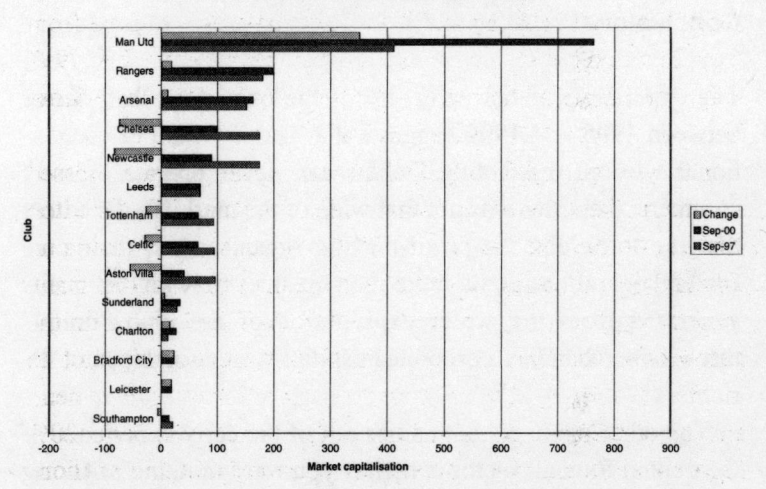

Source: *Financial Times*, September 1997 and September 2000

The Figure reveals that sharp declines in value were not limited to Football League clubs. In the Premiership, Aston Villa's valuation fell by almost 60% from £95 million to less than £40 million between 1997 and 2000. In 1997, the City had regarded Villa as one of the Premiership's top clubs, an established member of the "chasing pack" capable of challenging for the title and almost assured of a regular place in Europe. When these expectations were disappointed, the City punished it severely.

The major exception to this bleak picture was Manchester

United, whose market value over the period had almost doubled to £800 million, so that it dominates Figure 10.4.

But even in the case of Manchester United, there are doubts. Can it really be the case that a single club, no matter how strong, is worth almost as much as the combined value of the other 20 quoted Premiership and Football League clubs combined?

Conclusions

The experience of the early life of the quoted football sector between 1995 and 1999 suggests that perhaps the old conventional wisdom that football clubs can never operate as truly commercial entities was not that wide of the mark. To the extent that the top clubs are profit-making organisations, their core football operations do no more than break even, with the profits generated from the wider exploitation of the club "brand" through merchandise, corporate hospitality, sponsorship, and TV rights.

The other message that comes out of the early experience of the quoted football sector is that, if you were thinking of taking a punt on football by buying shares in a club, you should stick to quality. You would be well advised to avoid the Nationwide Football League altogether, and concentrate on the top rated Premiership clubs. Even there, you're taking a calculated risk. The value of any football club investment could be hit hard by managerial changes, player injuries, and the luck of winning one or two extra league points that could make the difference between lucrative European qualification or another season's toil in domestic football.

Many years ago, I was advised to stay clear of gambling and to invest any surplus funds in the stock exchange. "Gambling will lose money," was the sage advice; "but if you put your savings into the stock market, over time, they should grow."

I'm sure that the advice was well meant, but in football such normal rules do not apply. Investments in football clubs have tended to go down, while astute punts on football games can make money.

The truth is that both are forms of financial speculation. If you buy value in either type of market, you should make money. If you simply play hunches or back the favourite to win come what may, you are likely to end up a loser.

So how do you identify real value? As the 2000/01 domestic season got under way, that was the question that now occupied my attention.

11

Shopping around

Value Betting

Simply defined, value betting involves betting on events that you believe are more likely to happen than implied by the odds on offer. For example, if you think that the chance of a particular team winning the League is 50%, while the best odds offered by the bookmakers are 2/1 against, implying a 33% chance only, then you have a value bet proposition.

From this simple example, it can be seen that value betting has two aspects. The first is a forecasting system that can predict final results accurately. The second is shopping around for the best odds on offer. If the best price on offer is out of line with your own assessment of the likely outcome, then you may have a betting opportunity.

Pre-season prices for the English Premiership in 2000/01

Barely a month after the Euro 2000 final, it was time to get back to the bread and butter business of domestic club football. As I scanned my copy of *Odds On* for August 2000, I considered the odds quoted by the four leading fixed odds bookmakers against each of the twenty premiership teams to win the title, given in Table 11.1. In the Table, the best price (longest odds) is highlighted in bold, while the worse price (shortest odds) is shown in italics.

Table 11.1
Pre-season odds on the 20 Premiership Teams to win the League in 2000/01

Bookmaker	Ladbrokes	Hills	Coral	Tote	Odds percentages	
Team					Best	Worst
Man Utd	4-6	8-11	4-5	4-5	55.56%	60.00%
Arsenal	**4-1**	**4-1**	**4-1**	*7-2*	20.00%	28.57%
Liverpool	5-1	**11-2**	*9-2*	**11-2**	15.38%	22.22%
Chelsea	6-1	6-1	6-1	6-1	14.29%	14.29%
Leeds	*10-1*	11-1	**12-1**	*10-1*	7.69%	9.09%
Newcastle	**50-1**	40-1	*33-1*	*33-1*	1.96%	2.94%
Spurs	66-1	*50-1*	**80-1**	66-1	1.23%	1.96%
Aston Villa	66-1	80-1	**100-1**	*50-1*	0.99%	1.96%
West Ham	**200-1**	150-1	*80-1*	125-1	0.50%	1.23%
Everton	125-1	100-1	*80-1*	**150-1**	0.66%	1.23%
Sunderland	125-1	150-1	*100-1*	**175-1**	0.57%	0.99%
Middlesborough	**200-1**	**200-1**	*125-1*	**200-1**	0.50%	0.80%
Man City	350-1	250-1	*150-1*	**400-1**	0.25%	0.66%
Leicester	*250-1*	**300-1**	**300-1**	**300-1**	0.33%	0.40%
Coventry	350-1	**400-1**	*250-1*	350-1	0.25%	0.40%
Derby	250-1	**500-1**	*250-1*	350-1	0.20%	0.40%
Southampton	**500-1**	**500-1**	*300-1*	350-1	0.20%	0.33%
Charlton	750-1	*500-1*	**1000-1**	750-1	0.10%	0.20%
Ipswich	*1000-1*	*1000-1*	**2500-1**	*1000-1*	0.04%	0.10%
Bradford	*1000-1*	1250-1	**2500-1**	1500-1	0.04%	0.10%
				Total:	120.74%	147.88%

Source: *Odds On* magazine, Issue 97, August 2000, p.16

The odds bear a curious resemblance to one of those eighteenth century horse races where bookmakers simply pitched The Favourite against The Field. Like the City of London, the bookmakers clearly regarded Manchester Utd as the dominant team in England. Before the first ball of the new season was kicked, Man Utd were best priced at a remarkable 4/5 on with Coral and the Tote, implying that those firms thought they had more than a 50% chance of retaining the title. The best prices quoted on the remaining 19 teams in the League were equivalent to just under 1/2 on. So you could have backed every team other than Man Utd to win the title and you would have made a profit if any of them came good.

Looking down the Table, it becomes clear that the bookmaking fraternity thought that only four other teams stood a realistic chance of toppling Man Utd in the 2000/01 season: Arsenal, Liverpool, Chelsea and Leeds. The other 15 were "rags", offered at odds of 50/1 or longer, implying that the bookies' assessed their chance of winning at less than 2%.

Right at the bottom of the bookmakers' league table were Charlton, Ipswich and Bradford, all sides recently promoted from the Nationwide First Division. You could have got prices of 1000/1 or better on any of them to win the title. The bookies clearly agreed with Deloitte & Touche in seeing a widening gulf in class and resources between the First Division and the Premiership, and thought that the teams just promoted from the First Division would struggle to survive.

Converting odds to probabilities

To calculate the probabilities implied by the bookmakers' quotes, I converted the best and the worst odds offered by the four firms into percentage probabilities. This step is essential for value betting to facilitate the comparison between the bookmakers' prices and your own forecasts.

The conversion involves two steps:

Step 1: Converting to decimal odds. To convert conventional British odds to decimal odds, the odds against are divided by the odds for to derive a single number. So, for example, the odds of 6/1 about Chelsea to win the league offered by all four firms would convert into decimal odds of 6, while the odds of 7/2 against Arsenal offered by the Tote would equate to 3.5. Incidentally, the "decimal odds" or D.O. method is used by continental bookmakers such as Eurobet as the standard way of presenting their prices. It is also used by William Hill on their international website. This suggests that decimal odds may become an increasingly popular method of pricing up football bets. The continentals reckon it is easier for punters to calculate their winnings using this method, with the potential win being equal to the stake multiplied by the D.O. − a winning £1 bet on Chelsea yielding £6, £1 on Arsenal £3.50, and so on.

Where a team is odds on, as in the case of Man Utd, the decimal odds would be less than one. So the Ladbrokes quote of 4/6 on Man Utd to win the league would convert into a decimal odds quotation of 0.66 − a winning bet of £1 yielding just 66p.

Step 2: Converting decimal odds to probabilities. The probability is simply 1 divided by (1 + D.O.). Applying this formula, the odds of 6/1 against Chelsea would convert into a probability of 1/7 or 14.29%. The Tote odds of 7/2 against Arsenal would convert into a probability of 28.57%. Ladbrokes' odds of 4/6 on Man Utd convert to a probability of 60%.

Applying this formula, the percentage probabilities implied by the best and worst odds offered on Man Utd, the "chasing pack" of Arsenal, Liverpool, Chelsea and Leeds, and the 15 "rags" in the premiership are shown in Figure 11.1.

Figure 11.1
Probabilities of winning the League in 2000/01

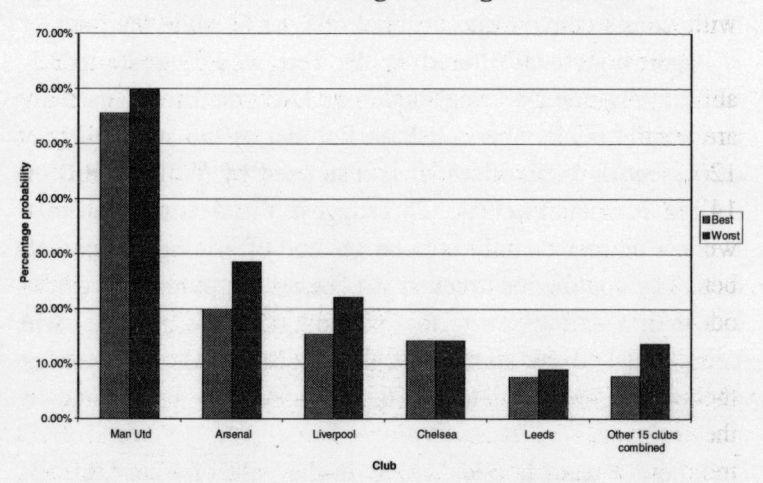

[Bar chart showing percentage probability (Best and Worst) for each club:
- Man Utd: ~56% / ~60%
- Arsenal: ~20% / ~28%
- Liverpool: ~15% / ~22%
- Chelsea: ~14% / ~14%
- Leeds: ~7.5% / ~9%
- Other 15 clubs combined: ~7.5% / ~13%]

Source: Adapted from odds quoted in *Odds On* magazine, Issue 97, August 2000, p.16

Figure 11.1 reveals that, in the case of every club other than Chelsea, there was a difference between the best and worst price on offer. Cumulatively, this difference is highly significant.

Why shopping around it so important

Figure 11.1 shows the probabilities implied by the best and worst odds quoted by the four leading high-street bookmakers. Only in the case of Chelsea were the odds quoted by all four bookmakers identical. In several cases, there was a wide variation in the odds against a particular the team's chance of winning the league. For example, if you were a Corals client, you would have secured short odds against both of the Liverpool teams compared to the prices quoted by the other three high street firms. It would have been naïve to bet on Everton at 80/1 with Corals when you could have got 150/1 with the Tote.

At the bottom of Table 11.1, I have aggregated the total probabilities implied by the best and worst odds on offer. The results are startling. The best odds sum to a combined probability of 120.74%. The worst odds have a combined probability of 147.88%. What this means is that, if you backed every team to win the league at the best available odds, you would need to bet £1.21 to win £1; while if you had taken the worst available odds, you would have wagered £1.48 to win £1.

Of course, this is a purely hypothetical example. No one in their right mind would back every team to win the league, as the bet would be bound to lose overall. But let's consider a more practical example. Suppose that, like many of the experts, you believe that the 2000/01 premiership was likely to be a three-horse race with just Manchester United, Arsenal and Liverpool as serious contenders. Let's suppose that you believe that it is 95% probable that one of these three teams with the title, with just a 5% chance that one of the other seventeen clubs may triumph.

If you took the worst odds on offer, you could not bet on this position. The combined probabilities implied by the worst odds would be 60% for Manchester United (the 4/6 Ladbrokes' quote), 28.57% for Arsenal (the Tote) and 22.22% for Liverpool (at Corals). The sum of these three is 110.8%, implying that you would lose more than 10p in the £ backing all three at these prices.

But if you take the best odds on offer, you could have a winning bet. The combined probabilities implied by the best prices about the three teams amount to 90.94%, or about 4% less than your assessment of the true likelihood that one of them will take the title. Taking these prices, you would have a value bet provided you could get one tax-free.

This illustrates the dramatic effect that shopping around can have. The effort would be worth approximately 25p in every £ bet on the English Premiership as a whole, and 20p in the £ for the three top-rated sides in the Premiership. And that is just among the four leading High Street bookmakers. If the sample were widened to include spread firms and Internet bookmakers, the effect would be even more dramatic.

When you take into account the fact that even the most successful professional gamblers, such as the legendary Alex Bird and Phil Bull, generated at best a 5% to 10% return on their speculative activities, you will appreciate that securing the best prices can make the difference between a profit and a loss. Indeed, the conclusion may be put even more strongly: *in devising and applying a successful speculative system, securing the best prices on offer is more important than developing a superlatively accurate forecasting system.*

In exceptional cases, it is possible to make profits by simply taking the best prices on offer without having to go to the effort of devising a rating system at all. Back in the early 1980s, an acquaintance of mine did just this, tramping around the bookmaking shops of south London and writing down the odds offered by each of them. Where the odds offered by one firm were significantly longer than its competitors, he simply placed a bet with that firm. The way he figured it, the oddsmakers were full-time professionals and were unlikely to get their prices consistently wrong. So if one firm was significantly out of line with the majority on a particular event, the chances were that, on that occasion, it had simply miscalculated the true probabilities, providing him with the opportunity for a value bet.

More often than not, the tactic paid off, and within six months my friend had won £30,000. At that point, he took a well-earned rest and travelled to Italy for a couple of months' holiday.

Securing the information

My friend's £30,000 profit had not come easily. He had expended a lot of shoe leather tramping around the betting shops, and then travelling to the nearest racecourse to avoid the dreaded betting duty. But it had been worth it.

But all good things come to an end. To his dismay, he discovered on his return that a new publication had hit the streets – the *Racing Post* – and, worse still, it had a comprehensive sports section that included all the early prices. With the "ricks" now transparent for all to see, it proved increasingly difficult to take advantage of them, as the first thing that any bookmaker would do would be to check the early prices in the *Post* and adjust his firm's quotes so that they were in line with the rest of the market. The information inefficiencies on which my friend relied had largely disappeared.

But not entirely. In an article in *Odds On* in April 2000, Derek McGovern passed on this piece of wisdom given to him by a London taxi driver. "There's a guaranteed way to make a profit on football betting," the estimable cabbie informed him, "if you see that Ladbrokes are shortest by a long way about a particular team, back that same team with a different bookie." The logic behind the system is that the Ladbrokes oddsmakers are better than those of any other firm, so are likely to have got their prices about right. Testing the system on a few games, McGovern discovered that it seems to work more often than not, and concluded that it might be worth following.

I'm not sure about the "back the Ladbrokes prices" method,

which may only last for as long as particular oddsmakers are employed by the Magic Sign. But certainly, where different bookmakers' prices are out of line, they cannot *all* be right. If you rate one higher than the others, it may be worth following their prices. If not, there may be an opportunity for arbitrage.

Such opportunities have undoubtedly increased with the development of spread betting and online gambling. You no longer have to walk several miles daily to get pricing information, as my friend did. You don't have to leave your home. All the pricing information you need is now at your fingertips. You can get it from Skytext or Teletext at the press of a zapper. The TV Text page numbers of some of the leading bookmakers are given in Table 11.2 below. If you do find a particularly attractive price quote on Teletext, then you can pick up the phone and place a bet to take advantage of the odds before they shorten.

There is still one problem with this method. It is that, unless you have an offshore account, you are likely to have to pay betting tax on winning bets. But at the dawn of the 21st century, even paying tax is an option that the sophisticated gambler can choose to forego. Whereas my friend in the early 1980s had to travel to a racecourse to be able to bet tax free, today we can all do it, by betting offshore over the Internet.

Table 11.2
Sources of Information:
Bookmakers' TV Text pages and websites

Firm	Information		Telephone		Website
	Teletext	Sky	Debit	Credit	
Fixed Odds					
Bet Direct	367 / 368	372	0800 211 222		
Coral	611/612/613	366	0800 12 67 25		eurobet.co.uk
Heathorns		363	01483 86 01 23	01484 41 81 81	heathorns.co.uk
Ladbrokes	605/606/607	373/374	0808 10 00 421		ladbrokes.co.uk
Stan James	633	364/367/368	0800 38 33 84		
Stanley					stanleybet.co.uk
Sunderlands			0800 78 36 849		sunderlands.co.uk
Surrey Sports	661	444 / 445	0800 07 22 421		
Tote	667/668	376	0800 82 55 50	0800 26 91 88	totalbet.com
William Hill	601/602/603	359/384	0800 44 40 40	0800 28 98 92	williamhill.co.uk
Internet					
Blue Square					bluesq.com
Demmy			0800 78 37 070	0800 91 78 080	sportsbet.co.uk
eurobet.co.uk					eurobet.co.uk
First Stake			0800 91 50 915	0800 91 50 915	www.firststake.com
Sporting					sportingodds.com
Ukbetting.com					ukbetting.com
Victor Chandler	620/621	286/287/288	0800 09 78 794	0800 09 78 797	victorchandler.co.uk
Spread Firms			Inquiries	Bets	
City	609	362/382	0207 86 15 000	0207 861 5000	cityindex.co.uk
IG	608	365/385	0500 913 911	0500 911 911	igsport.com
Sporting	604	381	08000 96 96 45	08000 96 96 02	sportingindex.com
Spread Ex	660	360	08000 52 65 75		spreadex.com
William Hill Index	600	359/383	0800 300 320	0800 48 05 00	willhillindex.com

12

Football betting online

The growth of online betting

Gambling is one of the fastest-growing Internet businesses. UK research agency MMD forecasts that worldwide online gambling turnover will increase from less than £1 billion in 1999 to £9 billion by 2002 and no less than £48 billion by 2010. This explosive growth is taking place even though betting on sports is illegal in most countries.

Commenting on the growth of online gambling in his article "Politics and the punter" in the *Financial Times* on March 18th 2000, respected sports journalist Patrick Harverson wrote that,

> "Even where betting is legal, many governments – worried about the loss of tax revenues – are trying to stop the activity migrating to cyberspace. But the legal and practical difficulties they face provide one of the clearest examples of how the Internet is undermining the traditional power and jurisdiction of government."

The article goes on to quote Senator John Kyl of Arizona, sponsor of an American Bill to ban online betting, contending that it was "unregulated, accessible to minors, addictive, subject to abuse for fraudulent purposes like money laundering, and evasive of state gambling laws."

Senator Kyl may well be right. But the practical problem that legislators face is how they can prevent the continuing growth of online betting. As a senior executive of one online gaming company commented, "if people want to gamble, they gamble. You can't wiretap and monitor everyone's personal computer."

It is now becoming clear that online betting is here to stay. Consequently the challenge for sports regulators is no longer how to prohibit gambling on sports. The regulatory task now is to ensure that the sports themselves are fair and open. This task can most easily be achieved if the rewards paid and penalties imposed upon coaches and players are so great that match fixing simply doesn't make sense. It seems likely that this is now the case at international and Premiership level.

Yet those who gamble on sports would do well to heed Senator Kyl's words of warning. The Internet, like the atom, can be put to good or bad uses. The weak and the ignorant may be seduced by its ease of access and use, and bet more than they can afford. But the intelligent speculator will draw on the Internet's immense resources to identify the most favourable markets and prices at which to trade, utilising the vast mass of information provided by the net to identify profitable opportunities.

The advantages of online gambling

It is not difficult to see why online gambling has experienced such dramatic growth. The potential advantages it offers over more traditional forms of betting include:

○ rapid and easy access to news and comment on forthcoming sporting events;

- easy access to the market-makers themselves, whose sites facilitate cheap and rapid betting – typical response times between opening a web page, placing a bet and securing bet confirmation are around two minutes, with the quickest sites taking less than 90 seconds;
- payments may be made electronically, without the need for the punter to do anything more than give details of a credit or debit card account into which winnings should be paid and losses deducted;
- Internet gambling offers the ability to place a bet at any time of the day or night from anywhere in the world, simply by plugging a mobile phone connection into a laptop;
- crucially, you don't have to pay tax charges on Internet bets. At the time of writing, online betting companies based in the UK, such as William Hill and Ladbrokes, offer tax-free offshore domiciles through which the British resident can bet without paying UK betting duty. The Internet has reduced betting duty to the status of a voluntary tax, payable only by those without access to the net, either because they are unaware of what it offers, or because they cannot afford it.

Naturally, this final feature of online betting is most unwelcome to the government. At the time of writing, the British Government has signalled its intent to replace betting duty with a general gambling tax that will also cover offshore and electronic betting. Options for collecting such a tax include requiring British residents to report all the winnings on offshore accounts in their tax returns, and stipulating that UK-based operators pay the tax on all bets that they accept, wherever in the world they are placed.

But there must be serious doubts as to whether either option is tenable. Do the gentlemen in Whitehall honestly expect gamblers to accurately report online bets that cannot be traced by Her Majesty's Inland Revenue? And if the government shifts the onus from the gambler onto the bookmaker, the chances are that the effect will be to displace betting activity from UK firms to offshore operators falling outside the long reach of the Treasury, resulting in a loss of revenue and employment to the UK.

So the most likely outlook is that online betting will continue to be tax-free. The position was summed up by professional horseracing gambler Alan Potts in his *Odds On* column in April 2000,

> "The future is here, and it works. In just two months, I have been converted into a technofreak who has his laptop plugged into the phone every afternoon that I don't spend out on the racecourse. I've turned over more money in the first two months of the year 2000 than ever before and not paid a penny in betting tax. I can only say that if you are still picking up the phone and accepting deductions, it's time to take the plunge. I can assure you that the one thing that an internet betting site never does is to ask you to hold on and then offer you '£25 at the price, and the rest at SP, sir'. At least when a website knocks you back, it's quick and utterly impartial."

Football information online

When I started writing this section, I thought I might be able to give a reasonably comprehensive rundown of the sources of information on football available on the internet. But the truth is the number of sites is so huge and changing so rapidly that such an endeavour would require an entire book in its own right, and such a book would rapidly become obsolete. So here are just a few of my favourite sites:

www.oddschecker.co.uk. A free site covering a whole range of sports, which gives instantaneous price comparisons on the odds quoted on major sports and racing events. By selecting a live TV game, you can rapidly access the odds being offered on a home win, draw or away win by leading bookmakers. At present, the site compares odds for major internationals and televised games only, its coverage is limited to about half a dozen leading bookmakers, and even for them the data provided may be incomplete. For example, when I checked its odds for the 2001 FA Cup, it only provided up-to-date quotes from William Hill, Sportingbet, Luvbet and UK Betting, with the columns for Paddy Power, Littlewoods, Ladbrokes and Victor Chandler all blank. Nevertheless, Oddschecker has the makings of a very useful service, enabling you to save time and effort in shopping around to get the best odds on offer.

www.osga.com. The Osga stands for the Offshore Gaming Association, which is the embryo of a self-regulating system for offshore and online gambling, and as such is greatly to be welcomed. It provides a comprehensive listing of online gaming sites including online casinos, provides a commentary on many of them, and endorses some of them. It is oriented towards sites operating out of the USA, but does include many of the British sites – for example, the Victor Chandler site gets a tick for "positive feedback" from customers – but some of the major UK sites are not even listed, with Ladbrokes, Eurobet and IG all notable by their absence. Osga also lists a number of gaming sites that the punter is warned to avoid as they have failed to pay out on winning bets. It invites surfers to fill out a complaint form for any site that they have used where they have experienced payment difficulties.

www.planetfootball.com. Planet football provides comprehensive information on football, both qualitatively in the form of news reports and quantitatively. The site provides vast amounts of raw statistics on team and player rankings, goals on target, successful tackles, completed dribbles, and just about anything else you can measure that happens in a football game!

www.racingpost.co.uk. The website of the *Racing Post*, the trade daily which includes an increasingly strong football section on its back pages, including an excellent column by Kevin Pullein. My own feeling is that the *Post* is more manageable in its printed form, as the huge wealth of information and analysis can be cramped and difficult to read online. Once you take into account the time and effort required to source and download information online, my feeling is that better value may be had anteing up £1.10 for the hard copy in the newsagents – unless of course you happen to be living in Timbuktu and can only reach the *Post* by cyberspace!

www.smartsig.com. The website of Stefan Perry's SMARTSig magazine, which I have always found a useful source of analysis and ideas – although, in keeping with Stefan's original mission for his magazine as providing an open forum for all thinking, it does include its fair share of dubious, unproven or just plain fallacious gambling theories as well! Unlike the *Racing Post*, SMARTSig does not publish its copy online, and the site is largely a publicity medium for the magazine, providing an index of recent articles in the magazine. It also helpfully provides a listing of bookmakers with their contact addresses and numbers, and provides links to other websites of tipsters.

www.soccerbase.com. Soccer base claims to be "the most comprehensive and up-to-date source of British football data on the Internet." I would challenge this assertion, as huge amounts of data are published by other football sites. But it cannot be denied that soccerbase is a useful source of information and analysis.

www.sportal.co.uk. Sportal provides match reports and results, and each game report includes a very useful summary of "match facts", which sets out the score, teams bookings and other statistics.

www.sports.com. For my money, Sports.com rates as perhaps the best and most comprehensive of all the sports sites that I have used. The site is well designed and easy to navigate, and gives access to comprehensive sports data. The live results section provides results and statistics of football games played in a wide range of leagues worldwide.

www.sporting-life.com. The old Sporting Life daily was closed some years ago, but the title lives on in this well-designed and informative website. Easy to navigate, with a menu that lists the various sports covered – soccer being the top-listed, ahead of racing and rugby – the site also provides information on pools and betting, and sports on TV. The site won a Website of the Year award in 1997.

www.weekendfootball.co.uk. Weekendfootball is another well-designed football site, which provides league tables and current form of each team for the last 12 games, and also gives information on weekend fixtures, comments on team form, and a section called "football betting" which offers links into the major bookmaking sites online. The site also includes a section entitled "results v. predictions", which sets out the site's own pre-match predictions and the actual results of all games in a way that is to be applauded for its transparency. Needless to say, if you want to get access to the predictions themselves before the game, a modest subscription fee is payable!

Conclusions

The online gambling revolution is here to stay and may be a precursor to an even more radical upheaval within the next five years when interactive television is introduced, merging the Internet with live TV coverage of football games. When this happens, at the click of a switch a gambler watching a live game on TV will be able to select a market on which to bet, find out the best price, and execute the trade within a matter of seconds.

A few short years ago, opportunities for betting on football were limited to "minimum trebles" paying 10% betting tax – a game that is impossible to beat as a practical proposition – or taking a punt on the pools. In the 21st century, the explosion in the range of markets, the choice of prices, and the number of operators both online and off mean that, by shopping around, an intelligent speculator can enjoy something close to a fair game when betting on football for the first time in history.

13

Online gambling sites

The High Street Bookmakers

So where are we to start in taking advantage of the Internet revolution to make some serious money from football betting?

The most obvious risk with online gambling is that you have no sight or sound of the counterparty with whom you place a bet, and, if the bookmaker is offshore, no means of collecting the bet should the counterparty fail to honour it. It is therefore imperative to bet only with reputable names who can be relied upon to honour their obligations. If you stray outside the established names, then my advice would be to start betting cautiously to ensure that they can be trusted to honour any debts. The good news is that, as matters stand, there are enough old-established names now trading online to get keen tax-free prices without the need to bet with an unknown firm.

William Hill was the first High Street bookmaker to launch an Internet betting website. It has since been followed by Ladbrokes. Both offer UK-based sites as well as overseas sites, and, if you bet on one of the offshore sites, you do not have to pay UK betting tax. Both the Hills and Ladbrokes sites highlight football as one of their main areas, and enable registered users to bet online by simply typing in their registered users number and password.

Leading sites operated by traditional High Street bookmakers include the following (in alphabetical order):

Ladbrokes. The UK site is www.bet.co.uk, the international site operated from Gibraltar is www.ladbrokes.com. A well-designed site from the world's biggest bookmaker, it offers tax-free betting across most sporting events on the calendar. It also provides helpful guidance on how to place different bets such as correct score, first goalscorer, half-time/full-time results and longer-term league and cup competitions. It is oriented towards the smaller stakes punter, requiring a minimum deposit of £5 and a minimum stake of £1. Betting is available between 9 a.m. and midnight each day.

Littlewoods: www.Bet247.co.uk. Although as a leading Pools operator Littlewoods are not strictly a High Street firm, I place them in this category as one of the traditional bookmaking firms that has spread its wings into online gambling. Like Ladbrokes, the Bet247.com site is tax-free, and, as you would expect given its parentage, it offers bets on football pools as well as conventional fixed odds. The site offers prices on the English football league, the Champions League, and the German, French and Spanish national leagues. Littlewoods also offer their own Golden Boot index on the top premiership goalscorer in the season, although my quick review of the odds on offer on this market indicated that they did not appear particularly generous.

Tote: www.totalbet.com. Totalbet.com, the online website of the Tote, is run in association with Sporting Life. Quite well-designed although wordy, it offers fixed odds betting on all UK televised football games as well as Italian Serie A, the Champions League, the UEFA Cup, and the 2002 World Cup.

When I checked over the site, its response times appeared to be slower than those of Ladbrokes or Littlewoods, and the site rules specify that "unless otherwise requested at the time of placing instructions, all bets will be settled as tax paid at an amount currently 2% for fixed odds and 9% for Tote pool bets," which suggests that better value may be had elsewhere.

Victor Chandler: www.victorchandler.co.uk. Chandlers are a long-established independent UK bookmaker, who broke the mould by being the first to locate overseas with the specific aim of enabling their clients to avoid UK betting duty. The site offers among the most imaginative graphics of any online betting site that I have visited. Of course, the more important question is whether it also offers good value! The good news is that the answer to this question is also broadly affirmative. Victor Chandler.com opens with the tempting offer of "permanent tax-free betting", provides a full range of match bets at fixed odds, and also contains previews incorporating statistics relating to each match. Single bets are accepted on matches in the English Premiership, the Spanish Primera Liga, Italian Serie A, and the German Bundesliga and on any Cup game, all internationals, and any game broadcast live on TV. For non-televised games in lower divisions, the minimum stipulation is a treble, although any game may be doubled with a live TV game. One disadvantage of the Chandlers site is that bets are not accepted in running. Chandlers also offer the "Asian line", which is a handicap issued for particular games to equalise the strength ratings of the two sides. For example, in a France v. Holland game, France might be given an Asian handicap of 0.5 goals, so that the Dutch would have an imaginary half goal start in the game. Any bet on Holland would win if the Dutch either won or drew the game, while the French would have to win outright. If France were playing a weaker side, such as Wales, they might be given an Asian line of 1.5 goals, so they would need to win by a margin of two or more goals for any bets to be paid.

William Hill: Hill's international site can be found at www.willhill.com, with their UK site address being www.williamhill.co.uk. Site design is not great, seeking to cram too much on to a single page, and bet procedures appear rather long-winded, with bet confirmation reportedly slow at times. The international site, operating out of Antigua, offers a betting service free of any tax or deduction. The odds on this site follow the European convention in being quoted in decimals, so that, for example, in the match between Dynamo Kiev and Manchester United played in the European Champions League on September 19th 2000, the odds quoted were 3.6 on Dynamo Kiev, 3.1 on the draw and 1.9 on Manchester United to win. The game ended in a 0–0 draw, so that a £1 bet on a draw would have returned £3.10 – a win of £2.10 plus the stake of £1.

The Internet Bookmakers

Blue Square: www.bluesq.com. Blue Square is the fixed odds offshoot of spread firm City Index, and offers a large range of bets on sporting events. Unfortunately, being based in the City of London, it is liable to pay UK betting duty, although at the time of writing this is levied only at 2.5%. It specialises in football match bets at fixed odds, quoting prices on the outright winner of all groups in UEFA tournaments.

Eurobet / Corals: www.eurobet.co.uk. Though linked with Corals and IG, Eurobet may more appropriately be seen as a separate stand-alone internet website. It is emerging as a leading European online betting service, quoting odds on games played in most major European leagues, including the domestic Portuguese league, in decimals.

First Stake: www.firststake.com. Bets can be placed online or by phone, and it claims to be one of the fastest sites available: "where else can you bet on the fastest goal of the new Premiership season and read about it seconds later?". It is a fixed odds site, and does not currently accept bets in running, although odds are updated at half-time. First stake offers tax-free betting, and its website is very easy to follow, offering the user a three stage process to bet selection: first, select a sport (e.g. UK soccer), then select a series (e.g. the Premiership) and finally select the event on which you wish to bet, such as a particular game. The screen then comes up with a range of quotes on the event of your choice and the bet is executed by completing and returning the quote sheet. I would rate this as one of the most user-friendly sites.

Luvbet: www.luvbet.com. The online branch of the Irish bookmaking firm O'Hallorans based in County Cork, this site offers tax-free betting from its offshore operation in Malta. It accepts bets in a number of currencies, focusing on racing and football, and also offers the option of placing of bets by phone rather than online. The range of football bets on offer is more limited than with specialist football sites such as Bet247 or Eurobet, as the site's focus is on racing. However, it does offer the standard range of fixed odds football bets on single games televised live so may be worth a visit to compare prices with those offered by the specialist football bookmakers.

Sportingbet: www.sportingbet.com. Operating out of the Channel Island of Alderney, Sportingbet.com has emerged as one of the leading players in the internet gambling revolution. Capitalised on the stock market at £200 million, it ranks as one of the largest bookmaking firms trading exclusively via the Internet. Sportingbet is a tax-free site and its site structure is similar to those of some of the spread firms, listing all sports on which it quotes prices and inviting the user to select one by clicking onto the sport of choice. It offers an extensive range of football prices including handicap bets, first and last goalscorer and correct score on the UK leagues and most major national leagues. Among the continental leagues quoted by Sportingbet are those of Portugal, Argentina, Denmark, Sweden and even Switzerland. It offers Asian handicap lines in addition to conventional outright result fixed odds bets.

Sporting Index: www.sportingodds.com. Sporting's fixed odds affiliate, and like its spread partner, it offers the key advantage of betting in running.

UKbetting: www.UKbetting.com. This London-based bookmaking site focuses on sports bets but levies a UK betting tax, currently at a rate of 7%, on them, which must make it uncompetitive compared to many other online bookmakers.

The Spread Firms

The spread firms' sites offer the punter to the opportunity to bet directly online. The tax charge is absorbed within the quoted buy/sell spread.

City: www.cityindex.co.uk. City's site asks the user to choose a "Super Group" such as football and then select a market on which you wish to bet, which might be a single game or a longer-term market such as Premier League points. Once you have made your choice, you simply click on the "go" icon to secure up-to-date prices. City's site is very useful for long-term markets, but it does not appear to be updated in running for match bets, and the final make-up on completed matches is reported more slowly than, for example, with Sporting Index. I suspect this reflects City's much smaller market share – latest estimates suggest that City has around a 10% share of the sports spread betting market, compared to 50% for Sporting. Having said that, City have never failed to give me excellent service and their prices are often highly competitive, so that I would recommend them to anyone seriously interested in spread betting.

IG: www.igsport.com. IG is the longest established of the spread firms, having originally opened for business almost 30 years ago when it first quoted spreads on gold prices – the IG originally stood for Index Gold. Perhaps reflecting its venerable old-age, IG's website seems somewhat more cumbersome and sluggish than its newest competitors, and you have to work your way through several menus to get from the home page to football quotes of your old choice. The football page rather awkwardly puts the markets on the right-hand side of the screen rather than the more conventional left-hand side adopted by City and Sporting. The effect of this is that they can be off the screen altogether, and can only be accessed by cursoring across. But the trudge through IG's spread pages is worth the effort, as the firm offers a number of original and innovative markets, and its match prices can differ significantly from those of its competitors, so that it often offers the best value available.

Sporting: www.sportingindex.com. Sporting is the largest specialist sports spread betting firm, and as one would expect offers a wide range of choice on football markets. Its site is well designed and easy to navigate, with the markets listed on the left-hand side of the screen on entry. This is a site that any serious football speculator is likely to access regularly, as Sporting provides benchmark prices on major UK and European football games and offers the most extensive range of markets of any of the spread firms, with the possible exception of IG.

Spreadex: www.spreadex.com. The latest entrant to the spread betting market, Spreadex concentrates mainly on financial spread betting, but do offer prices on all the leading football markets of Suprems, Total Goals, Bookings and team's Mini-Performances. However, as far as I could see, the site does not publish football quotes.

William Hill: www.willhillindex.com. William Hill's index website is the most disappointing of any of the spread firms. It does not provide live online prices, and its function seems to be more as a form of publicity advising surfers of how they can open an account. Annoyingly, the site refers the user to Hill's live prices quoted on Teletext. Hopefully "Britain's most respected bookmaker" as Hill's describes itself, will make more of an effort in the future. Perhaps they are waiting for the age of interactive digital TV when the net and television will become one.

14

Forecasting football matches

An Atlantic Superleague?

Over a number of seasons, there can be little doubt that the teams with the greatest financial resources are likely to do better. So we can predict with a degree of confidence that Manchester United will continue to be the best team in England for some time, while Arsenal, Chelsea, Liverpool and Newcastle United will constitute the chasing pack challenging for European honours. Should any of these teams suffer a decline in form, they have the funds to rectify the situation by recruiting new players or a new coach. Clubs such as Leicester City and Sunderland are almost certain to be playing "catch up", struggling to compete with the big clubs over a sustained period, and always vulnerable to losing their best players and coaching staff to them. With less money at their disposal, the smaller clubs are simply unable to offer as attractive terms to the finest talent.

The picture is even more extreme in Scotland, where Rangers, with a market capitalisation of around £200 million in September 2000, are more than twenty times as big as Heart of Midlothian, whose market cap was less than £10 million. Only Celtic could even start to challenge Rangers' financial clout. But with Celtic's market value just a third of that of Rangers, at around £65 million in September 2000, even they could be hard put to mount a sustained challenge to their Old Firm rivals.

Not surprisingly, Rangers have dominated the Scottish Premiership for over a decade, with their winning run interrupted only once by Celtic during the 1990s. By the beginning of the 21st century, the question that was increasingly being asked north of the border was whether you could have a viable competition when, at current club valuations, the leading club could buy up the rest of the League and still have change left over.

This is not just a problem for the rest of the League. It was also a problem for Rangers. The lack of competition they face in domestic Scottish football is providing inadequate preparation for much tougher challenges they encounter when they step up a class in European competition.

The commercial logic leads to an unavoidable conclusion. The competitive structure in Scotland is so ill balanced that, in its current form, the Scottish Premier League will always be a two-horse race between Rangers and Celtic. But, whichever team wins, they are unlikely to repeat past European triumphs, because the gulf in class between Scottish and European football is too great. In the medium term, it seems increasingly possible that Rangers and Celtic may leave the Scottish League to form a new Atlantic League with leading clubs from countries such as the Netherlands, Sweden and Portugal, where the domestic competition is similarly skewed and dominated by no more than three teams.

However, although over the course of a season, the Premier League will be decided between no more than two teams in Scotland and half a dozen in England, each team within the League still goes into each match with the genuine hope of getting a result. Even playing the likes of Manchester United away, the lowliest team in the English Premiership would hope to escape with a draw and a point.

So how likely is such a result? What techniques can be used to forecast the final result of any game before kick-off? And are these techniques sufficiently robust to form the basis of a successful speculative system that can be applied to gain an edge and make money through match betting?

Forecasting Matches through Goal scoring Rates

In an interesting paper entitled "Index Betting on Sports", originally presented at a 1990 International Gambling Conference in London, David Jackson and K.R. Mosurski hypothesised that the results of sporting events could be forecast by examining past scoring rates. "Many sports involving two teams, such as soccer and hockey, can be modelled as a Poisson process whereby teams A and B score goals at rates R_A and R_B respectively," they wrote. "In this simple model, the variable *Total Goals* is just the *sum* of two Poisson variables, and the variable *Margin of Supremacy* is just the difference of the same two variables. In other words, Total Goals is just the expected value of $(R_A + R_B)$ and the Margin of Supremacy is the expected value of $(R_A - R_B)$."

Could the Jackson–Mosurski method provide the basis of a winning system to identify when the spread firms' indices for Total Goals and Margin of Supremacy are out of line with the true expectation?

Evidently, Jackson & Mosurski felt it could. In the latter part of the paper, they give a practical example of how this could happen, drawing on the example of the England v. Ireland game played in the World Cup in Italy in July 1990.

Going into the game, England's average scoring rate per major international was 1.29, while Ireland's was 0.73. Applying their method, the predicted result was a margin of supremacy for England over Ireland of 0.56 (= 1.29 − 0.73), while the predicted Total Goals was 2.02 (= 1.29 + 0.73).

The pre-match spreads quoted on the game were 0.85–1.1 for the Margin of Supremacy, and 2.1–2.4 for Total Goals. As Total Goals was quite close to the expected outcome applying the model, there was no betting opportunity on this line. However, the bottom end of the Margin of Supremacy spread, at 0.85, was significantly higher than the statistically expected spread of 0.56 applying the Jackson–Mosurski method, signalling a profitable opportunity to Sell this index.

The game ended in a 1–1 draw, generating a profit of 0.85 × the unit stake for sellers.

Sadly, Jackson & Mosurski give no further examples of their method in practice, and, as all gamblers know, one swallow does not make a summer.

In principle, the method appears beguilingly attractive. It is simple to apply and appears to have sound theoretical foundations. In practice, it has one minor drawback. It doesn't work.

I tested the method to see how accurately average scoring rates going into a match predicted the actual outcome in 70 Premiership games played during the 1999/2000 domestic football season. Predicted Total Goals were the sum of the average goalscoring rates of the two teams going into the game, while the predicted Supremacy was the difference between them. The results of my test were not encouraging. The results are shown graphically in Figure 14.1 below.

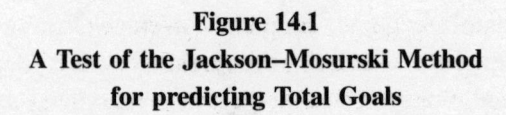

Figure 14.1
A Test of the Jackson–Mosurski Method
for predicting Total Goals

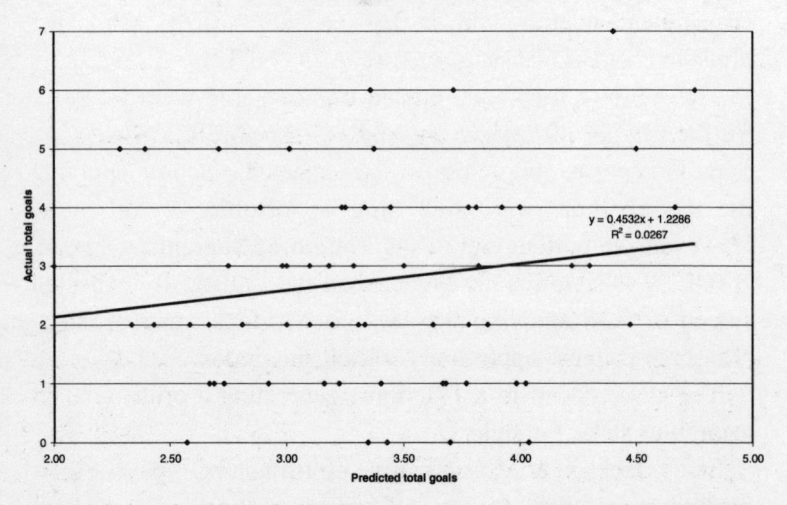

y = 0.4532x + 1.2286
$R^2 = 0.0267$

The horizontal axis of the Figure shows the predicted number of goals to be scored in a game, applying the Jackson–Mosurski method. The vertical axis shows the actual number scored. The straight line measures the best fit linear relationship between them. It can be seen by visual inspection that the relationship is extremely weak – in fact, the correlation coefficient (R^2) is less than 0.03, indicating that there is less than a 3% relationship between the two. This is statistically meaningless. In simple English, there is no relationship.

The picture is little better if the Margin of Supremacy is considered, as shown graphically in Figure 14.2.

The best fit that I could find was between the actual margin of supremacy – shown here on the horizontal axis – and the predicted margin as a function of the Home Team's Average Scoring Rate playing at Home minus the Away Team's Average

Scoring Rate playing Away. This is shown on the vertical axis. Again, the best fit trend line between the two indicates a very weak correlation – in this case, of 7.26% – which is statistically meaningless.

Figure 14.2
A Test of the Jackson–Mosurski Method for predicting Supremacy Margin

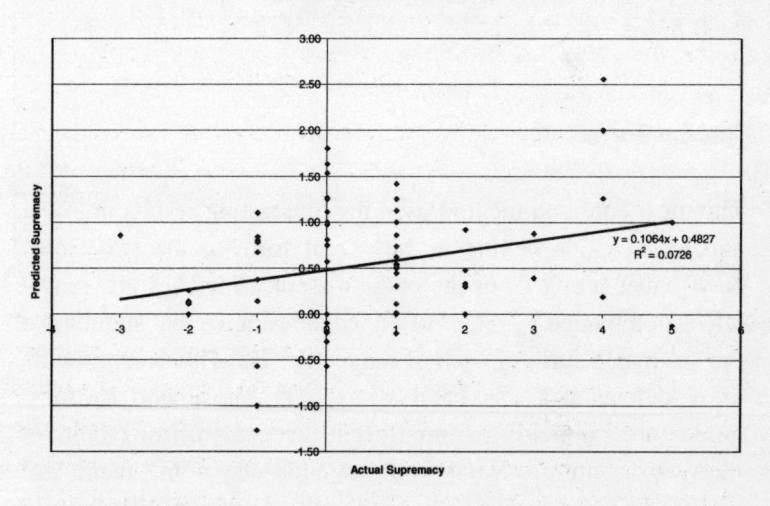

[Scatter plot with Predicted Supremacy on vertical axis and Actual Supremacy on horizontal axis; trend line equation: $y = 0.1064x + 0.4827$, $R^2 = 0.0726$]

It should also be borne in mind that, most of the time, the pre-match spreads quoted by the index firms were pretty much within the range indicated by past scoring rates. When they fell outside the range, and I bet against them, more often than not I ended up as the loser.

Responding to my dwindling betting bank and the hard evidence of my statistical analysis, I rapidly abandoned the Jackson–Mosurski approach. It is possible that a more extensive test would generate more encouraging results; but I doubt it. A more likely conclusion is that pre-match scoring rates are a weak and unreliable predictor of actual scoring rates during a game. This conclusion seems to hold whatever pre-match scoring rates are used.

Another conclusion of my research was that, where the linesmakers' spreads varied from the Jackson–Mosurski line to a significant degree, more often than not they beat it – suggesting that they were adjusting statistically generated forecasts in a way that accurately reflected the particular circumstances of each game.

Recent form

The most common method used for forecasting results in Pools and Fixed Odds betting is the recent form of the two sides. Newspaper previews of the coming week's matches are generally accompanied by tables of all league fixtures that summarise the six-match form of each of the teams. The Tables mark wins as W, defeats as L (loss) and draws as X. Those who use form guides are implicitly assuming that a recent run of results is likely to continue. So if you saw that the home team had achieved six successive wins on the trot – WWWWWW – while the away team had suffered six successive losses – LLLLLL – you would probably forecast a home win. Similarly, if you noted by scanning the form guides that the two teams playing in a particular game had each drawn four of their last six games, showing a pattern something like XWXXLX, you might conclude that there was a better than average chance that the forthcoming game between them would also end in a draw, making the game a banker for the Treble Chance Pools.

I must confess that I've not subjected the "recent form" theory to as rigorous a statistical analysis as the Jackson-Mosurski model. But on the face of it, it seems to have a number of weaknesses. It says nothing about the comparative strength of each of the teams played in the last six games. It does not indicate any special circumstances applying to those games or to the upcoming fixture, for example in terms of the absence of key players through injury, which might influence the result. Adherents of this approach could claim at best that it provides an indication of the overall result, but not the margin of supremacy or total goals likely to be scored, so that it could not be used for spread betting.

My conclusion is that crude recent form analysis of the type given in newspaper previews provides at best a rough first cut for match forecasting. The fact that those who use this approach continue to plug away week after week without evident success, rather than retiring on their winnings to a well-earned rest in the Caribbean, makes one suspect that, even as a rough first cut, the method is not particularly effective.

Elo type systems

Forecasting systems based on the methods first devised for chess ratings by an American physics professor, Dr Arpad Elo, address many of the weaknesses of the crude "recent form" approach. Elo developed his method to rate the comparative strength of different chess players, with the differences in rating applied to predict the probability of victory by the higher rated player. His method is explained in his book, *The Rating of Chessplayers, Past and Present*, and has been applied to many other games and sports.

Although chess is as near to a game of pure skill as it is possible to find, actual outcomes will never be precisely the same as those predicted by the Elo ratings. Players are improving or deteriorating all the time; one player may prepare better for a particular game, or simply be more alert on the day; a higher rated player may not perform up to the rating differential if he or she takes the lower rated player for granted; and so on. Nevertheless, the Elo rating is now widely accepted as providing an accurate predictor of the outcome of chess games and matches.

Elo ratings are not fixed, but increase if a player wins steadily, and decrease if he or she loses consistently. The ratings are adjusted by a factor reflecting the difference between the two players going into the match, but not by the full differential.

Applying the Elo approach to football, you might award ten points for a full goal differential between two sides. For example, if two teams went into a match both rated as 100, and you allowed five points (or 0.5 of a goal) to reflect home advantage, then the home side would have a pre-match rating of 105, and the away side 100. If the result ended in a 2–0 victory for the home side, then it will be performing 15 points above its pre-match rating. If you immediately adjusted the two sides' rating by the full difference between the actual outcome and the pre-match rating, then you would add 15 points to the home team's pre-match rating to bring it to 115, while simultaneously subtracting 15 points from the away team to reduce it to 85.

In practice, it would be wrong to adjust the rating by the full extent of the variance, and an adjustment factor might more accurately be set at a quarter or a fifth.

An interesting application of the Elo approach to football can be found in Chapter 8 of Drapkin & Forsyth's 1987 book *The Punter's Revenge*. The method proposed by Drapkin & Forsyth envisages that "each side contributes a fixed proportion of its rating into a 'kitty' or 'pot'." They go on to comment that, "our investigations reveal the best results appear to be obtained with the home team putting 7% of its strength into this pot and the away side contributing 5%." So, in the case of a game between two sides both with a pre-match rating of 100, the home team would put 7 units into the pot and the away side 5. The total value of the pot is 12 units (7 plus 5). The system is "winner takes all" with the pot split if the game is drawn. Applying this system:

- in the event of a home victory, the home team would be rated at 105 after the game (= 100 − 7 + 12) and the away team at 95 (= 100 − 5);
- if there was an away win, the away team would have a post-match rating of 107 (= 100 − 5 + 12) and the home team 93 (or 100−7); and
- if the game was drawn, the pot would be split so the home team would have a post-match rating of 99 (= 100 − 7 + 6) and the away team 101.

I can report that the system is reasonably easy to apply, and appears to generate superior forecasts to either the Jackson–Mosurski "goalscoring rate method" or the crude "recent form" method.

15

Points mean Prizes

A practical problem with Elo-type systems is that they require significant time and effort to develop. And for domestic football there may be a much easier way of rating the comparative strength of different teams – the good old League Table.

But can the difference between two sides in league points be used to forecast likely match outcomes? If so, how reliable would such forecasts be? To try and answer these questions, I drew on data given in Bill Hunter's Forth Dimension website, which provides statistics on more than 1,500 English Premiership and Football League games played in the 1995/96 season. These statistics provide information on the difference in league points between the two teams going into each game and the final result.

Figure 15.1 shows the difference in league points between the two sides going into each game. It approximates what statisticians term a "normal distribution". As might be expected, the average pre-match difference in league points was zero, but there was a wide spread around this average. In almost half the games played, the difference between the two sides was small, falling in a range of plus or minus 10 points. But there was a fair spread outside this range. At the extreme ends of the range, there were just over 50 league games where the home team enjoyed an advantage of thirty or more points over the away team going into the game. There were also about 50 games where the away side had a similar points advantage.

Figure 15.1
The pre-match difference in league points in 1,500 football games played in the English Premiership and Football Leagues in 1995/96

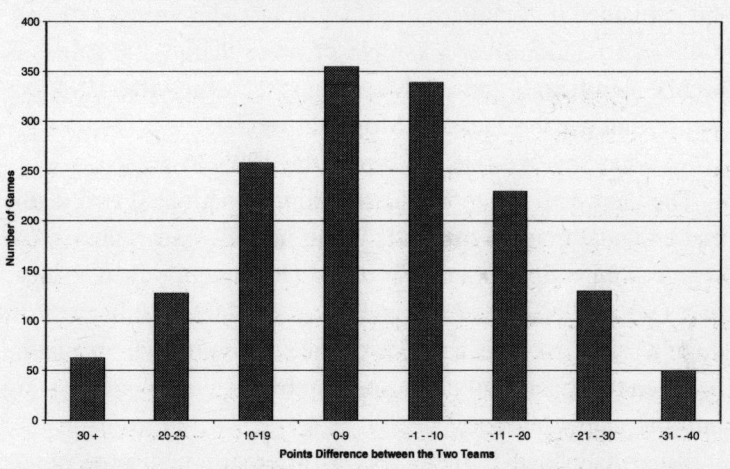

Source: Adapted from data published on Bill Hunter's *Forth Dimension* internet website

Points differentials and the probability of home wins

First of all, I regressed the percentage of home wins against the pre-match points advantage (or disadvantage) enjoyed by the home side over the away side. The results are shown in Figure 15.2.

The Figure indicates that there is a positive relationship between the two. In other words, the greater the pre-match league points advantage enjoyed by the home team, the more likely it is that the home team will go on to win the game.

The relationship between the two indicated by the correlation coefficient (R^2) is statistically significant, at 0.42. This indicates that 42% of the variation home wins is explained by the difference in pre-match league points between the home and away sides. Of course, this still means that 58% of home wins are explained by factors *other* than points supremacy. But still, a 42% correlation over a sample of more than 1,500 games is highly significant, and in sharp contrast to the weak relationship found for the Jackson–Mosurski model.

So what was the relationship in the 1995/96 season?

The answer is given by the trendline equation. If two teams had an equal number of points going into the game, then x, the league points differential, was zero. The equation then reduces to y (the probability of a home win) = 0.448. In other words, there was, on average, a 44.8% chance of a home win in a game between two teams with an equal number of league points going into the game.

What happened if there was a difference in league points going into the game? The x parameter of 0.0053 indicates that, on average, each league point advantage enjoyed by the home team over the away team going into the game translated into an increase of just over half a percent (to be precise, 0.53%), in the home team's expectation of victory. Conversely, if the away side enjoyed a points advantage over the home side going into the game, then the likelihood of home victory would *fall* by about 0.5% for each league point supremacy enjoyed by the away team.

Figure 15.2
The relationship between the probability of a home victory and the pre-match points difference in 1,500 English league football games played in 1995/96

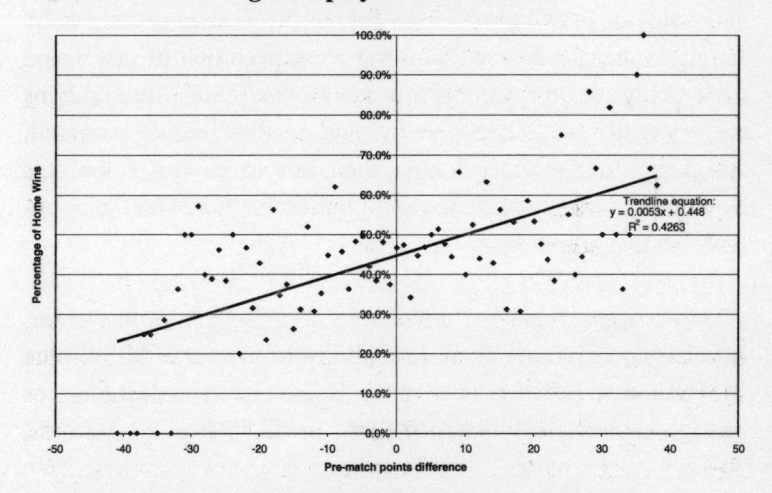

Trendline equation:
$y = 0.0053x + 0.448$
$R^2 = 0.4263$

Source: Adapted from data published on Bill Hunter's *Forth Dimension* internet website

Let's take three examples to show how this works:

Case 1. The Home Team has 48 league points going into the game while the Away Team has 38 points. Home Team points advantage = 10 points (or 48 − 38). Home Team probability of victory = 44.8% plus (10 points × 0.53%), or 5.3%. Adding 44.8% to 5.3% indicates that the Home Team has a 50.1% expectation of outright victory going into the game. The Home Team should be an even money shot going into the game. If you can get odds of 3/2 against a Home Win, fill your boots!

Case 2. The Home Team has 38 league points going into the game while the Away Team has 48 points. This is the reverse of the above situation. The Home Team points deficit is now 10 points. Home Team probability of victory = 44.8% *minus* (10 points × 0.53%), or 5.3%. Taking 5.3% away from 44.8% indicates that the Home Team has an expectation of just under 40% going into the game. Now the Home Team's true odds of victory really are 3/2, and you would need to find odds against which are significantly longer than this to have a value bet. Something like 2/1 against would tempt me to bet on the home team in this situation.

Case 3. Home Team net advantage of 15 league points going into the game. Home Team probability of victory = 44.8% plus (15 points × 0.53%), or 7.95%. Home Team expectation of outright victory = 44.8% + 7.95%, or 52.75% going into the game.

These three examples illustrate how, in principle, you could generate Home Win odds just by plugging in the pre-match points difference between the two sides and calculating the equation 44.8% + (0.53% × Points Difference) to pull out the best estimate of the probability of a Home Win. If this probability differed significantly from that implied by the bookmakers' odds, then you would have a value bet, based on the results of the 1995/96 season.

Points differentials and the probability of away wins

The next question was whether there was a similar relationship between the percentage of *away* wins and the pre-match points advantage (or disadvantage) enjoyed by the away side. The results are shown in Figure 15.3. As in the case of Home Wins, there does appear to be a statistically significant relationship between Away Win probability and the pre-match point differential. Figure 15.3 shows a negative relationship between the two – the greater the pre-match league points advantage enjoyed by the home team, the less likely it is that the away team will win. And no matter how great the points advantage enjoyed by the away side going into the game, there is never much more than a 50% or even money chance of an away victory.

Figure 15.3
The relationship between the probability of an away win and the pre-match points difference in 1,500 English league football games played in 1995/96

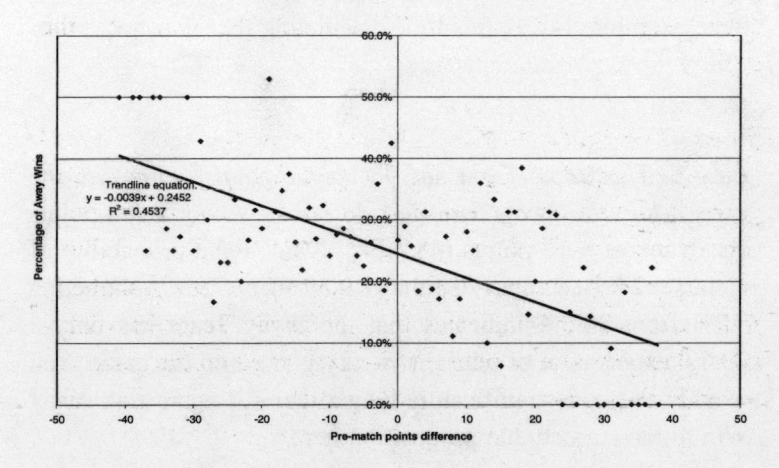

Trendline equation:
$y = -0.0039x + 0.2452$
$R^2 = 0.4537$

Source: Adapted from data published on Bill Hunter's *Forth Dimension* internet website

The relationship between the pre-match league points differential and the probability of an away win indicated by the correlation coefficient (R^2) is statistically significant, at 0.45. So 45% of the variation of away wins is explained by the difference in pre-match league points between the two sides.

The regression for the 1995/96 season shows that, if two teams had an equal number of points going into the game, then there was a 24.5% probability of an away win. If there was a difference in league points going into the game, each league point advantage enjoyed by the away team translated into an increase of 0.39% in the team's expectation of victory. But if the home side enjoyed a pre-match league points advantage, then the chance of an away win would *fall* by 0.39% for each one-point supremacy enjoyed by the home team.

To see how this would work in practice, let's run through the three examples again, this time calculating the away win probability:

Case 1. The Home Team has 48 league points going into the game while the Away Team has 38 points. Away Team points disadvantage = 10 points (48 − 38). Away Team probability of victory = 24.5% minus (10 points × 0.39%), or 3.9%. Subtracting 3.9% from 24.5% indicates that the Away Team has only a 20.6% expectation of outright victory going into the game. You would need odds significantly longer than 4/1 against an Away Win to have a bettable proposition here.

Case 2. The Home Team has 38 league points going into the game while the Away Team has 48 points. The Away Team now has a points advantage of 10 points. Away Team probability of victory = 24.5% *plus* (10 × 0.39%). Adding 3.9% to 24.5% indicates that the Away Team has more than a 28% expectation of victory going into the game. If you could get 4/1 odds against this result, you should make money over time always assuming you are betting tax free.

Case 3. Home Team net advantage of 15 league points going into the game. The Away Team probability of victory now falls to 24.5% minus (15 points × 0.39% = 5.85%), or just 18.65%, equivalent to approximately 11/2 against in conventional odds.

Points differentials and the probability of draws

The final question that I addressed was the relationship between the percentage of draws and the pre-match points differential. The results are shown in Figure 15.4.

The result that emerges from Figure 15.4 is, in its way, just as remarkable as that for the Home Wins and the Away Wins. *There appears to be no statistically significant relationship between the difference in league points going into the game and the chance of a draw!*

Figure 15.4
The relationship between the probability of a draw and the pre-match points difference in 1,500 English league football games played in 1995/96

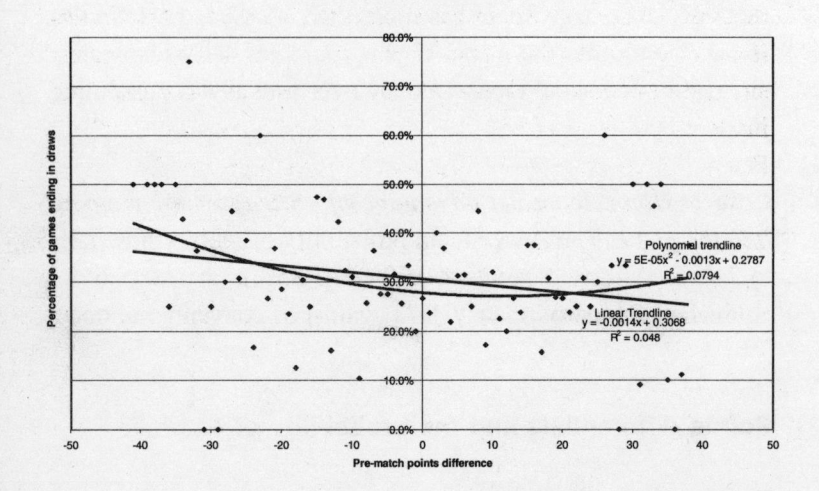

Polynomial trendline
$y = 5\text{E-}05x^2 - 0.0013x + 0.2787$
$R^2 = 0.0794$

Linear Trendline
$y = -0.0014x + 0.3068$
$R^2 = 0.048$

Source: Adapted from data published on Bill Hunter's *Forth Dimension* internet website

At first, I was so surprised by this result that I thought it must be a mistake. Of course, I reasoned, there would be no *straight-line* relationship of the type identified for Homes and Aways – the chance of a draw should go up, the closer the two teams were in league points and position going into a game. So perhaps this relationship is better described by a polynomial rather than a linear equation?

So I ran a polynomial regression. But, as Figure 15.4 shows, the result is much the same. The correlation coefficient (R^2) goes up slightly from 0.048 to 0.079, but it is still statistically insignificant. Furthermore, if anything, the polynomial shows the chances of a draw *go down* slightly, the more closely matched the two sides are!

No wonder the Pools people love the Treble Chance draws! Figure 15.4 shows that they are pretty much random and unpredictable, and to the very limited extent that they can be predicted, it looks as if the chances of a draw are lower, the closer the sides are in league points going into the game! All those poor, innocent punters who have spent long hours pouring over the Form Guides have been completely wasting their time!

No matter how you work it, the chance of a draw is between 28% and 30% going into any league game!

16

The Pride and the Passion

You may have gathered by now that I am a great believer in the power of statistical analysis to generate reliable estimates of the probability of particular events. But you will also have noted that statistical analysis has its limitations. Impressive though the relationship is, differences in league points going into the game still account for less than half of the difference in match results. Now, it is possible that someone smarter than I am could plug more variables into a model to improve on the accuracy of these pre-match forecasts. But in my experience it is difficult to achieve an accuracy of much more than 50%, no matter how sophisticated the forecasting methods.

Why? Because the relative strength of two sides going into a game is only a part of the match equation. At least as important are factors that cannot be captured by statistical models – the pride and the passion of the players who take the field, their morale and physical fitness on the day, and the role that chance can play in the unfolding on-field drama.

Psychological Momentum in Football

In an article entitled *A Game of Two Halves* published in his SMARTSig magazine, Stefan Perry examined football games played between a home underdog and a strong away favourite – say a Southampton v. Man Utd clash. In the article, Stefan tested the hypothesis that, if no goal is scored in the first half of these games, then "the balance of probability swings away from the top club and the poorer team are now a more favourable prospect" as they gain in confidence.

He found evidence in support of this theory by showing that, during the preceding two seasons, the home underdog gained an average supremacy of 0.025 of a goal in the second half. He concluded that such situations could offer the prospect of profitable betting, as the average half-time spread quoted by index firms in favour of the away favourite seemed to be approximately 0.8–1.0. Selling the away favourite at half-time therefore could be a profitable strategy.

On further examination, the data given in the article provided more general evidence of psychological momentum when a home underdog faces an away favourite. Overall, the team doing well at half-time tends to improve its position in the second half. The data in Stefan's article is shown graphically in Figure 16.1 from the perspective of the pre-match away favourite.

The chart shows that, if the away favourite is losing at half-time, it will on average lose by a larger margin at full-time. If it is winning at half-time, it will on average add to the half-time lead in the second half.

But where there is a strong home favourite, the psychology of the half-time break seems to be different, as shown in Figure 16.2. The Figure shows the second half supremacy of a home favourite over an away underdog for a range of half-time situations. It reveals that, whatever the half-time result – whether the home favourite is winning, losing or drawing – it tends to improve its position in the second half. Interestingly, the improvement *is least* if the sides go in 0–0 at half-time – in this case, the average

Figure 16.1
Second half goal supremacy of an away favourite (AF) over a home underdog

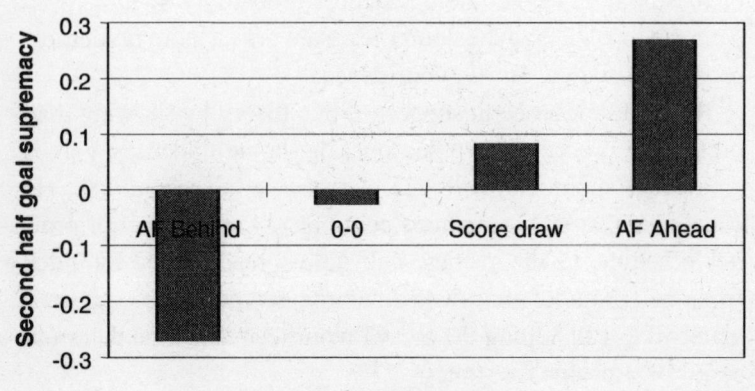

[Bar chart showing Second half goal supremacy on y-axis (-0.3 to 0.3) vs Half time score on x-axis with categories: AF Behind (≈ -0.27), 0-0 (≈ -0.02), Score draw (≈ 0.08), AF Ahead (≈ 0.27)]

Source: Based on data given in Stefan Perry's article "A Game of Two Halves", *SMARTSig* 5.03, March 1998

second-half supremacy of the Home Favourite was just 0.4 goals. This perhaps suggests that, until the first goal is scored, sides may be as concerned to avoid conceding a goal as they are to score one. Where the sides go in with an equal score at half-time, or where the Home Favourite is ahead, the Home Favourite's second half supremacy averages around 0.6 goals.

But the most startling point that emerges from Figure 16.2 is the dramatic improvement in the Home Favourite's performance when they are *behind* at half-time. Here, the average second-half supremacy of the home team is more than a full goal. This suggests that the home side is more strongly motivated when it is behind at half-time than in any other match situation. Why? Possible reasons could be that the home players respond to a half-time dressing-room roasting from their manager, or simply that their own self-respect spurs them to play harder so as not to let down home supporters in a match against a manifestly weaker side.

Figure 16.2

Second half goal supremacy of a home favourite (HF) over an away underdog

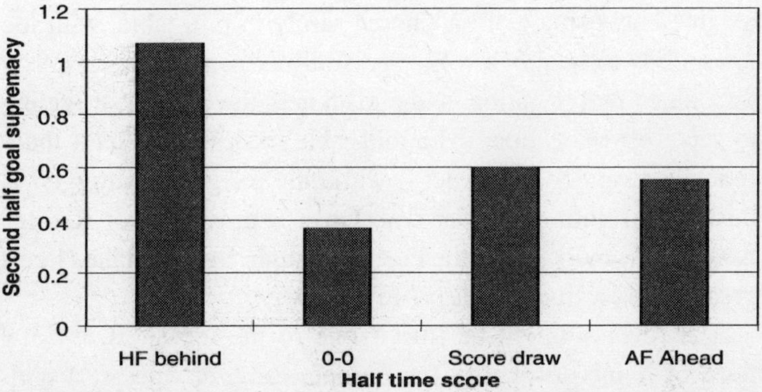
1.2
1
0.8
0.6
0.4
0.2
0
Second half goal supremacy
HF behind
0-0
Score draw
AF Ahead
Half time score

Source: based on data given in Stefan Perry's article "A Game of Two Halves", *SMARTSig* 5.03, March 1998

Whatever the explanation, the goalscoring patterns given in Figures 16.1 and 16.2 are clearly not explicable by simple pre-match power ratings.

The Fox and the Hare: Positive Motivational Factors

According to legend, although the fox is faster than the hare, in any race between them the hare will get away nine times out of ten. The fox is running for its lunch, while the hare is running for its life.

The same phenomenon can sometimes be observed in football. Particularly towards the end of a season, matches are played which have little meaning for one side, while for the other the result may have immense consequences. An example might be a game between a team anchored safely in mid-table, with too few points to qualify for Europe and too many to be seriously threatened by relegation, and a team near the bottom struggling to stave off relegation. The mid-table team is the Fox – theoretically stronger and faster – while the relegation struggler is the Hare, fighting for survival. On a simple "Power Rating" basis, you would expect the Fox to triumph. But often the Hare's greater motivation enables it to get away.

The reverse might be true if one of the top sides, in vital need of points to qualify for Europe, came up against a mid-table team in the closing stages of the Premiership. Now the Fox and Hare factors may be working in harness; power and motivation are both with the Favourite, who may go on to win by a margin greater than would be predicted by the difference in league position alone.

There are a number of other factors that may work to motivate one side more strongly than another, and they are all worth taking into account when seeking to forecast the outcome of a game.

1. *The Revenge Factor*.
   If, in the previous game between them, one side was unlucky to lose to the other – or, even better, if it was robbed of

victory by what the players might regard as unfair refereeing, such as a harsh penalty decision – then that experience will be seared into the team's collective memory. It will mean they will come out buzzing in the next game, keen to score a decisive victory against their adversaries to set the record straight.

2. *The Backlash Factor.*

   The backlash factor is a wider application of the revenge factor. Revenge applies to just one team who are seen as having won or drawn unfairly. A backlash can occur against any team.

   A classic case occurred in September 2000. Rangers, thrashed 6–2 by Celtic in the Old Firm derby early that month, then went on to secure a lacklustre 1–1 draw against Dundee. Heavily criticised by the press – and no doubt by coach Dick Advocaat – their players went into their first European Champions League fixture against Sturm Graz of Austria on September 12th fired up and determined to prove their critics wrong. The result was one of the most one-sided games I have ever witnessed, as the Scottish champions, inspired by outstanding performances from Ronald de Boer, Allan Johnston and Michael Mols on his comeback, decimated the Austrians 5–0.

   The moral of the story is that, where a class side has had a temporary downturn in form and fortune, it would be unwise to bet on it continuing. Sooner or later, some unfortunate team is likely to feel the backlash.

3. *The Insult Factor.*

   Where a team, or its players, believe they have been denigrated by members of the opposition, they will go out onto the park wanting to prove a point. The extra motivation provided by perceived insults may lead to them performing above their pre-match rating.

4. *Derby Games*
   Derbies between local rivals capture revenge, backlash, insults and all the other psychological motivators that can influence the result of a game in a single contest. The long history between sides like Rangers and Celtic, Liverpool and Everton, Manchester Utd and Manchester City, Newcastle and Sunderland, means that players and fans are up for these games like no other. League position and form goes out of the window as the derby takes on a meaning of its own, independent of the competitive context in which it is played.

   It is notoriously difficult to predict the result of these games.

Letdown and Exhaustion: Negative Motivational Factors

Whereas factors such as the desire to avenge real or perceived insults tend to be positive motivators driving teams to play above themselves, teams can also be affected by negative motivators.

One of the most common is the *Letdown Factor*. This factor typically applies when a meaningless match is sandwiched between two more important contests – say a midweek League game between an FA Cup match and a European fixture. In such cases, many of the leading clubs might field a second string XI to rest some of their top players. Even where this does not apply, first choice players may not be up for the game physically or psychologically, and lack keenness at crucial times during the game.

A wider application of this phenomenon is the *Exhaustion Factor*. If mid-winter league matches are postponed due to bad weather, and a club does well in Cup and European competitions, it can face end-of-season fixture congestion. All top Premiership sides now operate squad systems, anticipating the immense demands placed upon them by contemporary match schedules. Even so, it is likely that players will not be as fresh or fit as the season nears its close. For all their professionalism, when they need to dig deep, they may simply not have the reserves of energy left.

At the end of the season, the Exhaustion Factor could tell against the top sides facing a series of fixtures in different competitions compressed into a short timescale. If so, it may tell in favour of less highly rated teams with an easier programme.

Conclusions

It is difficult to predict the overall effect of these positive and negative motivational factors on the outcome of a game before the kick-off.

I have known some who have tried – for example, knocking 0.3 goals off the predicted margin of supremacy if a star player is out injured. But these sort of events are very difficult to model statistically.

In some cases, it is possible to visualise the effects of Pride and Passion before the game begins, but even here your pre-match vision may be widely at variance from what then unfolds on the field of play – or at least, mine is!

So do we just have to accept that we cannot use motivational factors to predict the outcome of a game? Absolutely not. While it is difficult to use these factors to arrive at a pre-match forecast, they can be immensely powerful aids to betting in running. If a Home Underdog is out for revenge, coming off a sequence of bad results, and determined to prove its worth, while a more highly-rated Away Favourite is suffering from fixture exhaustion, then you may suspect before the game begins that the Underdog could overcome the 1.3–1.6 Supremacy price quoted about the Favourite. But you don't have to take a position yet. You can await further confirmation in running. Watching the game live on TV, you see nothing to contradict your pre-match views. And when, after 40 minutes, the home team goes ahead, you know it is time to act.

Anyone who has played football for even the humblest park side is familiar with the phenomenon. Up against a more fancied team, we do not rate our chances going into the game. But a goal, even one scored against the run of play, lifts our spirits and as the game goes on, the self-belief of our side gradually gets stronger.

The spread firms find it difficult to take account of factors such as these, and generally move their lines only in response to the actual score so far, according to the formula:

$$Current\ quote = current\ score + (opening\ quote \times number\ of\ minutes\ left\ to\ play\ /\ 90)$$

True to form, when you phone up at half-time, you find the spread firm has applied the formula to mechanically crank out its latest mid-price as

$$0.275 = -1 + (1.45 \times 45/90)$$

Quoted a spread of 0.2 – 0.4 on the Home Team's supremacy, you happily buy at 0.4 – knowing that you have 0.6 points in the bag as you strike the bet, with the Home Underdog ahead 1–0 at the break. You also know that, if anything, an Away Favourite behind at half-time tends to fall further behind in the second half. And you believe that all the motivational factors are in favour of the home team, as is evident from their greater speed and sharpness on the field of play.

If that is not a value bet, I don't know what is.

17

Bookings and biases in gambling behaviour

Why do people gamble?

In his book *Paradoxes of Gambling Behaviour*, Dutch psychologist Willem Wagenaar sought to explain what motivates people to gamble. As most gamblers lose more than they win, it appears irrational that people choose to gamble at all.

Wagenaar identified a number of factors that help explain the apparent paradox. First, and most obviously, gambling is a form of entertainment. Therefore money spent on gambling is no different from money spent on other forms of leisure activity such as going to the cinema or a football match.

This first motive may explain a modest flutter, but it does not account for larger bets when gamblers place significantly greater sums at risk than they would dream of spending on an evening's entertainment. Wagenaar found that, while gamblers as a whole lose more than they win, they do not *expect* to lose when they place a bet. And they value the money that they expect to win more highly than the money that they have already lost. They also place a greater value on the remote expectation of a big win than on the probability of a small loss. As Wagenaar puts it, "the utility of losing small amounts is neglected, compared to the utility of winning large amounts." It is this that accounts for the enduring popularity of the National Lottery and the Pools, which offer the tempting prospect of a huge win in return for small initial bets.

Now, most of those who play the Lottery or the Pools would readily acknowledge that, overall, punters must lose more than they will win, if only because the operators have to take a cut from the pool. But at the same time, they would probably contend that, for any individual, this negative statistical expectation is irrelevant. Either you stand to win a lot or to lose a little; you cannot lose the "average" amount. As any particular event is unique, the average statistical outcome will never materialise.

So while a Pools punter would accept that those gambling on the Pools must bet more money than they win, he or she would not accept that it is impossible for *them* to win. After all, someone must win. Indeed it is precisely the chance of the life transforming win that persuades punters to keep filling in their Lottery or Pools forms, week after week, even after suffering a long sequence of losses.

A further reason for this phenomenon identified by Wagenaar is that gamblers typically suppress the memory of losing. "Good memories are more available than bad memories", he writes. This factor leads many gamblers to overestimate the probability of winning.

These hypotheses were borne out by the findings of a series of experiments that Wagenaar conducted with blackjack players in Dutch casinos during the 1980s. He found that players generally wanted to win, "but a complicated structure of false or incomplete knowledge, and irrational beliefs, prevents them from achieving this goal." Among the fallacies characterising the blackjack players Wagenaar studied were:

- selective memory: remembering pleasant experiences (winning) and forgetting unpleasant experiences (losing);
- attributing losses to external factors, such as the playing decisions made by the player at last base, rather than the inherent negative odds;
- confirmation bias – remembering events that confirm fallacious beliefs;
- false correlation – for example, placing reliance on lucky charms associated with previous successes;
- flexible attribution – "there is a tendency among gamblers to contribute successes to one's own skill, and failures to other factors."

The Gambler's Fallacy

The picture of the average gambler that emerges from Wagenaar's research is not flattering. Avaricious, ill-informed, impulsive, too idle to do proper research, and unaware of the true value of money, the poor punter is almost doomed to lose before they start. The probability of a big win is hopelessly overestimated, while the initial money put into the pot is hardly valued at all. So gamblers quite literally throw good money after bad. "People like the kick, the excitement, maybe the suspense, of possibly winning a large amount," Wagenaar writes. "The public is generally fascinated by lotteries with enormous prizes and low probabilities".

If there is one central fallacy that emerges from Wagenaar's research, it is that *most gamblers would rather accept a high probability of a small loss than a small chance of a bigger loss, irrespective of the likely returns*. In a phrase, they are "risk averse". Nor are these bias limited to gambling. Kahneman, in his study *Psychological Biases and Risk Taking in Financial Decisions,* finds that this bias occurs in all forms of financial speculation and investment.

But can the small number of rational speculators, who play *with* the probabilities rather than ignoring them, use this bias to their advantage?

There is some evidence that Gambler's Fallacy results in mispricings that an astute speculator can on occasion turn to profit. For example, it is a well-established finding that the odds offered against favourites are often closer to the true probabilities than the odds offered against outsiders. Bookmakers know that gamblers seeking a big payoff for a small outlay may follow rank outsiders, leaving stronger contenders poorly supported, and will adjust their prices accordingly. In spread betting, the line can sometimes be biased upwards if the spread firms find that there is a bias to Buy rather than Sell on lines such as the Total Goals index. The Total Goals line, as I discovered in the Holland v. Yugoslavia game, offers limited upside to sellers but much greater potential downside exposure.

However, biases against Favourites in big horse races, or in favour of buying rather than selling the Total Goals Index, are generally not large enough to offset the spread firm's margin or the fixed odds' bookmaker's overround. In other words, while you might lose less backing Favourites than Outsiders, or selling rather than buying Total Goals, you would still stand to lose, in the long term.

The bookings index

Is this also true of the Bookings Index?

The index has emerged as the third most popular market on

the spreads after Suprems and Total Goals, and it is easy to see why. Awarding 10 points for each yellow card issued to a player, and 25 points for any red card, it offers the enticing prospect of continuous excitement through the game. More cynically, it could be argued that this index appeals to the worst emotions of the football crowd as a mob baying for players' blood, urging the referee to respond to even the most innocent missed tackle with a sending off.

But whatever your interpretation of this line, there is no doubt that most of the fun will be on the "buy" side. An episode of the BBC2 Series *Jackpot* entitled "Red Lolly, Yellow Lolly" shown in August 2000 revealed how one professional gambler used this piece of intelligence to his advantage.

Jackpot tells the story of two gamblers betting on the Bookings Index – or, more accurately, of one solitary gambler, Bert Peters, and a couple of friends, John and Les. John and Les are "a couple of East End car dealers, who've only been into spread betting for about the year, but they already feel there's good money to be made."

As the programme unfolded, it became clear that John and Les were gamblers, more excited by the action than the promise of regular profits. They also appear to be victims of the Gambler's Fallacy, valuing their winnings more highly than their losses and generally betting on the Buy side to limit their downside exposure. Their approach involved buying the bookings index in games officiated by referees whom they regarded as harsh. More often than not, this approach appeared to cost them money.

Bert Peters was different. Bert was a professional speculator who " hadn't had a job since 1962", and "had been banned from casinos around the world for card counting" (now where have I heard that before?). While John and Les were buyers of the

Bookings Index, Bert was a seller. "He gathers statistics from hundreds of games, looking for patterns and loopholes, errors by the spread firms" reported the voiceover. "He specialises in the football bookings market. In three and a half years, he has won over £600,000."

The method that Bert used was ludicrously simple. It involved selling Bookings Index. "Contrary to what people believe, referees actually don't like going to their pocket," commented Bert; "they don't like waving a yellow card; they would prefer a nice friendly match."

Bert had confirmed this hypothesis by checking the actual record of bookings made over 300 matches. Early in the programme, he is shown selling bookings for an amount of almost £3,000 per yellow card (or £300 per point) in a Chelsea v. Leeds match. In a particularly bad tempered encounter, the Bookings Index made up at 90, costing Bert almost £10,000. Worse was to follow, as the cameras caught Bert taking a huge hit on what was reported as his worst game for two years, when he lost £15,000.

With the Peters bankroll now some £25,000 lighter, it was inevitable that he would be forced to cut back the size of his stake. The programme showed him betting at a level closer to £200 per point or £2,000 per yellow card. But with the football authorities recommending a more lenient approach by referees, at last his luck begun to change, and he succeeded in clawing back a profit of £7,500 on the next game.

But even this apparently did not make Bert entirely happy. He was now worried that, with fewer bookings, buyers might dry up, and the spread firms would start adjusting their lines downwards, eliminating his opportunities for profitable sell trades.

As the programme came to an end, Bert was considering

other lines to attack, to the considerable consternation of the IG football linesmaker Patrick Jay.

Should Patrick really have been worried that a solitary professional gambler such as Bert was able to make a make money from bookings, or indeed any other lines? I would say not. Provided Patrick was able to achieve an approximate balance between buying and selling activity, his firm, IG Index, stood to make money no matter what the final result. In fact, it could be argued that the activities of a professional gambler selling the line might actually help IG. As most of the fun and excitement in the Bookings Index is on the Buy side, and as buying also has less risk and potentially greater returns on any single game considered in isolation, more punters are likely to be buyers than sellers. This could lead the spread firms to adjust their lines upwards higher than the true statistical expectation. But an upward adjustment by itself would not help the firm to balance its books. To do that, they actually need some sellers. So by drawing in one or two professional speculators such as Bert Peters, who are capable of absorbing the occasional big loss, spread firms would reduce their own risk exposure and so help to smooth their income stream through time.

18

The Golden Boot and other speciality markets

"That Petrol Emotion" and other propositions

Sadly, "Red Lolly, Yellow Lolly" never did reveal which new football market had attracted the attention of professional gambler Bert Peters when he feared his action on the Bookings Index might dry up. But I have a suspicion that it was not the various proposition bets offered by the index firms, such as the "Behind Enemy Lines" or "Dad's Army" indices quoted by Sporting Index on the England v. Germany game in Euro 2000.

Looking at the growing number of speciality bets on offer, I am reminded of the advice given to the itinerant gambler Sky Masterton by his father as he set out on his journey in life. The old man's advice to his son was very simple. If one day some man came to him with a brand new deck of cards on which the seal was unbroken, and offered to bet that the jack of spades would jump out of the deck and squirt cider in Sky's ear, he should not accept the bet, "for as sure as you do," his dad advised him, "you are going to get a ear full of cider."

In other words, never accept a proposition bet, no matter how massively the odds appear to be in your favour, because whoever is setting up the proposition knows a lot more about the true odds than you do.

The essence of the proposition bet is that it should be fun, even bizarre, so our interest is tickled by it and we are almost tempted to accept it, just to see what will happen. But if there's real money involved, no matter how little, you should never treat any bet as fun. You should always seek to assess the true odds before deciding whether to accept the proposition.

The problem with proposition bets is that it is difficult for the punter to carry out the research necessary to arrive at an accurate assessment of the odds in the time available. Consider, for example, Sporting's "Petrol Emotion" Index of Saturday September 16th 2000, quoted at an opening spread of 125–140. The Index was offered as a one-off as Britain emerged from a petrol crisis caused by a nationwide refinery blockade in protest against fuel taxes. Both the nature of the index, and the wide spread quoted on it, provide a clue as to its target market. The Petrol Emotion Index comprised six components, all referenced to fuel and strikes: for example the 'Cole-Powered' component awarded 25 points if Andy Cole scored and Manchester Utd also won, while 'Crude' gave 25 points for each sending off in the Premiership. The full index composition is given in Table 18.1 below.

Table 18.1
Composition of Sporting's 'That Petrol Emotion' Index

Component	Scoring
"Panic Buys"	15 pts if Ginola, Carbone, Bellamy, Wiltord substituted
"Cole-Powered"	25 pts if Andy Cole scores and Man Utd win
"Winter of Discontent"	10 pts per yellow card given by Jeff Winter in Charlton game
"C-5"	50 pts each Premier team scoring 5 or more
"Crude"	25 pts each Premiership sending off
"Un-lead-ed"	10 pts any Premier team taking the lead & not going on to win

Source: Racing Post, September 16th 2000

Don't worry too much about the individual components. The point is that, with such a complex index, it would be difficult if not impossible for any punter to quickly acquire the mass of statistical data needed to establish whether or not the 125–140 opening line represented an accurate forecast of the likely make-up. And that is precisely the purpose of the exercise. Indices like these are targeted at inveterate gamblers desperate for a fix, and not at all bothered about statistical expectation.

But you can bet your bottom dollar that the oddsmakers setting the line *have* undertaken such an assessment. And what's more, the wide spread between the buying and selling quotes should mean they stand to win even if their assessment is slightly wrong.

The Golden Boot 1994/95

A possible exception to the general rule that you should stay away from speciality markets is the Golden Boot Index. Originally introduced by Sporting Index in the early 1990s, this Index invites gamblers to take a position on which strikers in the Premier League will score most goals. I would rate this market as somewhere between the mainstream football markets such as Suprems, Total Goals and Bookings for which historic data is readily available and relevant, and the Proposition Bets where past data is either not easily available, or not relevant as a basis for forecasting.

At one level, the Golden Boot is simply a proposition bet enabling gamblers to put their money where their mouths are in the age-old debate about "who is the best striker in England?" But at the same time, statistics and other information can be utilised to help answer this question, so it isn't quite up there with Sky Masterton's cider-squirting jack of spades. You can make money on the Golden Boot Index if you can interpret publicly available information more efficiently than the rest of the market.

The Golden Boot Index as originally devised by Sporting in the early 1990s was framed around eight of the top Premiership strikers. It has evolved since, but as the index in its early years was very simple, it usefully illustrates the principles underlying the market. In the 1994/95 season, Sporting awarded 75 points to the player scoring most goals, 50 points to the runner-up, and 25 points to the third-placed. The remaining five players each had a final make-up of zero.

The evolution of the 1994/95 Golden Boot Index for the top four strikers at defined dates is shown in Figure 18.1. For the record, the other four strikers listed in Sporting's Golden Boot Index that year were:

- Juergen Klinsmann (Spurs): Klinsmann started the season well, but had been comfortably overtaken by Alan Shearer and Robbie Fowler by Christmas and was then really only challenging for a third-placed position;
- Ian Wright (Arsenal): Wright was afflicted by injury and suffered an up-and-down season, never really challenging the leaders;
- Les Ferdinand (QPR), and
- Matt Le Tissier (Southampton): both leading the strike-force of clubs that spent most of the season battling against relegation, and neither got the service they needed from indifferent midfields. They started low and went lower before expiring with zero make-ups.

Figure 18.1
The Evolution of the 1994/95 Golden Boot Index

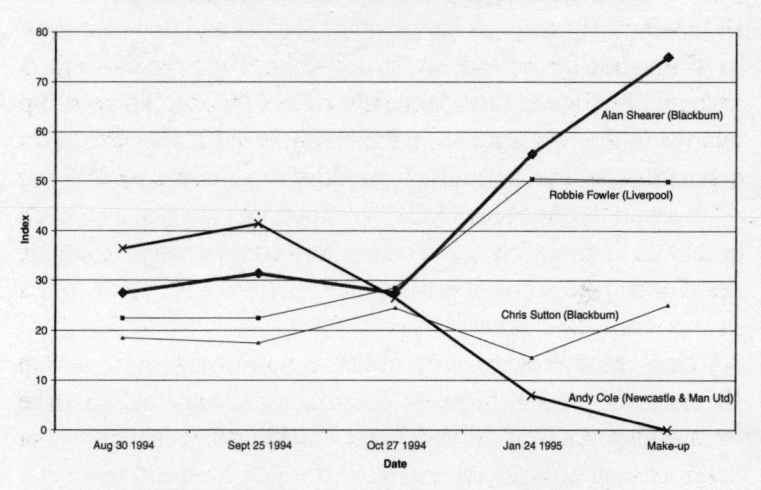

[Chart showing index values from Aug 30 1994 to Make-up for four players: Alan Shearer (Blackburn), Robbie Fowler (Liverpool), Chris Sutton (Blackburn), and Andy Cole (Newcastle & Man Utd)]

Source: Sporting Index quotes at the dates indicated

Figure 18.1 reveals that the early leader in the 1994/95 Golden Boot stakes was Andy Cole, then of Newcastle United, who transferred to Manchester United during the season. Cole showed outstanding early-season form, scoring four league goals by the end August and seven by the end of September, at which point he led the field. But he then picked up an injury and did not play over the Christmas period. During his lay-off, Alan Shearer of Blackburn Rovers and Liverpool's Robbie Fowler continued to score consistently, and by January were well ahead of chasing pack with 20 goals apiece. Shearer went on to take 1994/95 Golden Boot award as the top scoring striker, with Fowler finishing as runner-up.

By January 1995, with their combined total of 109 points on the index, there was little value in buying either Shearer or Fowler, as the maximum make-up on the two combined was only 125, implying a risk/return ratio of 109/16. In other words, you would have effectively been taking odds of 7 to 1 on (risking £7 to win £1) as early as January that Shearer and Fowler would have finished as the top two goalscorers. This payoff seemed to me at the time not to adequately reflect the risks of possible injuries to the two leaders, or the possibility that they might be overhauled by late hat tricks scored by the chasing pack.

The story of the 1994/95 Golden Boot does suggest a number of factors that may be worth taking into account when deciding whether to take a position on such an index:

1. Don't plunge in too early. Wait a couple of months to assess the early season form of the striker and his club. Anyone backing Andy Cole early in 1994/95 would have taken a cold bath after he withdrew with injury before Christmas.
2. On the other hand, don't wait too long either! As shown in Figure 18.1, most of the value in Shearer and Fowler had disappeared by January, with several months still left to play. Certainly they were well ahead of the pack by then, but this was fully discounted in the prices offered. The best time to open a position on the Golden Boot might be somewhere between October and Christmas – well enough into the season to have assessed form and fitness, but not so far in that the competition has already been decided.
3. In deciding whether to bet, take account not only of the form and fitness of the individual strikers, but also the fortunes of their team. If an outstanding striker is playing in front of a struggling midfield, it may be that his goalscoring opportunities start drying up as they revert to defensive mode in an effort to stave off relegation. On the other hand, even a striker of average quality can do well if supplied by a quality side striving for league honours.

4. Back strikers playing for successful sides. The leading goalscorer in the Premiership is likely to come from one of the highest scoring teams, and highest scoring teams are likely to finish at or near the top of the league. As at January 1995, Blackburn Rovers were riding high at the top of the Premier League, with only Manchester United and Liverpool within striking distance of them. It is no coincidence that the winner of the Golden Boot was Blackburn's top marksman, Alan Shearer, while the runner-up was Liverpool's Robbie Fowler, and the third placed striker was Chris Sutton, also of Blackburn Rovers.

The Golden Boot and Dynamic Duo, 2000/01

The element of chance and skill intermingled in the Golden Boot, and the fact that it aligns the gambler's fortunes with those of his or her favourite striker, have made it one of the most popular long-term football markets. Versions of the Golden Boot are now offered by all the index firms. Sporting's original index has been expanded to include 16 players, of whom eight are awarded points, ranging from 60 for the winner to 5 for the eighth-placed striker. City's is the closest to the Sporting Golden Boot index of 1994/95, giving points only to the top four named strikers in a group of ten, ranging from 50 points for the winner to 10 for the fourth-placed among ten named players.

As both these indices are based around individual players, they can be affected by freak injuries or losses of form. IG's Dynamic Duo Index reduces these risks by offering prices for the combined total of goals scored by the two leading strikers of each team, so that, if one is injured or in poor form, there is always the chance that the other may more than compensate by continuing to score well. Like City's Golden Boot index, IG's Dynamic Duo index is framed around ten participants and offers 50 points for the winners, 30 for the runners-up, 20 for third place, and 10 for fourth place. As it is quoted about two players, it is an intermediate bet between the total number of goals likely to be scored by particular teams and punts on individual players.

This is reflected in the quotes offered on the index at September 17th 2000. Although Manchester United's strike force of Andy Cole and Dwight Yorke had not started the season particularly well, with only three goals between them (all scored by Cole), their joint index remained high. This undoubtedly reflected IG and the market's belief that, with the power of the Manchester United midfield to supply them, it was highly likely that the duo would come good later in the season, and not be far off the pace by the end.

Figure 18.2
IG's Dynamic Duo Index, September 17th 2000

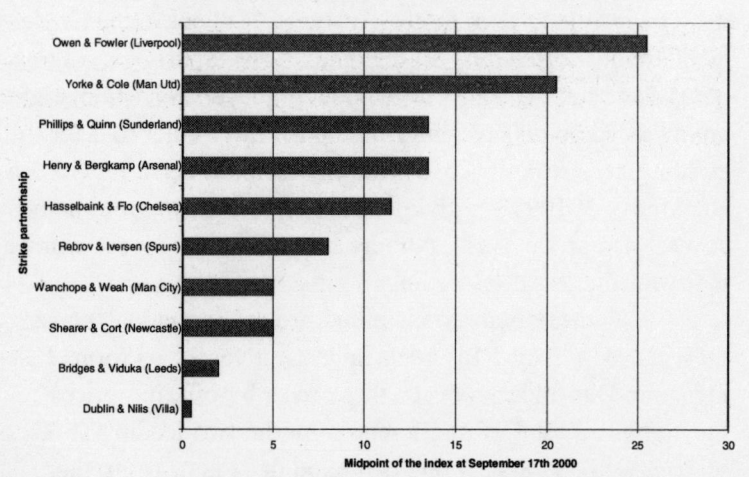

Source: IG Index, September 17th 2000

IG's Dynamic Duo quotes as at September 17th 2000 are shown in Figure 18.2.

However, simply playing as the strike force of a strong club does not itself guarantee success. If strikers are out of form, they are likely to be dropped or even transferred: threats that perhaps hung over Messrs Viduka and Bridges at Leeds, who had failed to open their accounts by September 17th. And if the team itself is not doing as well as expected, this too will be reflected in the prices, as in the case of Hasselbaink and Flo at Chelsea, a club that in September 2000 had just sacked manager Gianlucca Vialli after a poor start to the season. Perhaps the best combination is a settled strike force in a team performing up to expectation, so it is no surprise to see Liverpool's Michael Owen and Robbie Fowler heading the index in mid-September 2000. With six goals between them (all scored by Owen), they were already two ahead of the chasing pack, with little danger of being disadvantaged by a struggling midfield.

One final point is that arbitrage opportunities may arise between the different indices. At times opportunities arise to profitably cross-trade individual Golden Boot indices, IG's Dynamic Duo, and the Total Goals lines offered on different clubs by different firms.

19

Measuring Success

How do you know if you've got a winning system for betting on football?

Naturally enough, you hope that any betting system you use will generate a steady stream of profits. If it does, you can be fairly confident that you can make money by speculating on the game.

But, in the real world, successful speculation is rarely like that. More often, it is a series of fluctuations upwards and downwards around what should, over time, be a winning trend. But over any short period even a winning system may generate losses.

The risk is that, when you first apply it, the system generates losses before it starts to grind ahead. If you are not aware of the normal fluctuations that occur in most successful speculative activities, then there is a risk that you will abandon the system as a lost cause before it starts making money for you.

Conversely, there is a risk that you hit upon a losing system and experience "beginner's luck" in the shape of a few early wins. This could be even more damaging to your bankroll than the first case, if an early run of luck sucks you in and induces you to gamble ever greater amounts. Eventually, your luck will turn and losses will start to accumulate. If you don't recognise beginner's luck for what it is, there is a very real risk that you will persevere with a losing system, throwing good money after bad long after you should have cut your losses.

The good news is that I have devised a far less costly method of working out when you should abandon losing systems, and when you can be confident that a system you are using is a winner. In this chapter, I will describe the principles underpinning this method and give three examples of how it can be applied.

How the Method Works

The method involves five steps:

1. Keep a record of every bet made, the win or loss associated with it, and the cumulative win or loss to date.
2. Calculate the average win or loss per bet, equal to the cumulative win or loss divided by the number of bets placed.
3. Compute the standard deviation, or the extent to which the actual result of each bet fluctuates from the average.
4. Calculate the standard error, which is the standard deviation divided by the square root of the number of bets placed.
5. Finally, the average result is divided by the standard error to arrive at the "t" statistic.

Put simply, the higher the value of t, the more confident you can be that your profits are the result of skill or a genuinely viable system rather than just luck. If the average win is three times the standard error, generating a t statistic of 3, you can be 99% confident that your winnings are the result of skill rather than luck. If t is 2, you are still more than 95% certain of the viability of the system. With a t value of 1, you are just over 80% certain, and if t is 0.7 you are around 75% certain.

For most punters, keeping a record of wins is easy enough and calculating the average is also straightforward. The most difficult stage in the process is Step 3, which involves calculating the standard deviation of the win. The way I calculate the standard deviation of the wins (or losses) to date is by using the @STDEV function in Excel or @STD function in Lotus 1-2-3. Typing in @STDEV and specifying the range will return the standard deviation automatically.

An alternative to computing the standard deviation is to graph the cumulative wins and losses over time, to get a picture of what is happening.

Case 1 – The Sage of Omaha

To illustrate how the method works, my first case study is the investment record of the man who is quite possibly the most successful investor of the twentieth century, Warren Buffet, the Sage of Omaha. Through his investment vehicle Berkshire Hathaway, Buffet has consistently outperformed the Stock Market. He has done so through the application of basic value investment principles and a homespun philosophy set out in his annual *Letters to Shareholders*.

Buffet possesses an almost idealised vision of the benefits of free market capitalism. "The market, like the Lord, helps those who help themselves," Buffet informed his shareholders in 1982. "But, unlike the Lord, the market does not forgive those who know not what they do." Consistent with this philosophy, Buffet takes infinite pains in selecting his stocks and regards himself as a co-owner alongside the senior executives running the firms in which he invests.

A typical Buffet investment was in the Nebraska Furniture Mart, chaired by the redoubtable Rose Blumkin. As Buffet told the story to his shareholders in 1983, hers was a classic rags to riches story. "About 67 years ago Mrs Blumkin, then 23, talked her way past a border guard to leave Russia for America," Buffet wrote. "She had no formal education, not even at the grammar school level, and knew no English. In 1937, after many years of selling used clothing, Mrs Blumkin had saved $500 with which to realise the dream of opening a furniture store, the Nebraska Furniture Mart. She met every obstacle you would expect (and a few you wouldn't) when a business endowed with only $500 and no locational or product advantage goes up against rich, long entrenched competition."

The way Buffet told the story, she triumphed simply by perseverance, hard work and offering the customers far better deals than any of the competition. She continued to work a seven-day week through her nineties, and on her 100th birthday, as Buffet reported with obvious approval, the candles on her cake were worth more than the cake itself.

Buffet obviously has a taste for the simple things in life, and his approach to investment is equally straightforward. "Our long-term economic goal," Buffet informed his shareholders on March 14th 1984, "is to maximise the average annual rate of gain in intrinsic business value on a per share basis."

So how successful was Buffet in achieving that objective, and how confident can *we* be that his results were due to something more than their chance?

The growth of Berkshire Hathaway over the ten-year period between 1982 and 1991 is shown in Figure 19.1. The Figure reveals that, over that period, the value of shareholders' funds rose from just over $500 million to more than $7 billion, a compound growth rate of around 30% per year. By the end of the decade, Buffet was generally reckoned to be one of the three richest men in the world, and his early shareholders had prospered with him.

Figure 19.1
The Growth of Berkshire Hathaway Equity, 1982–1991

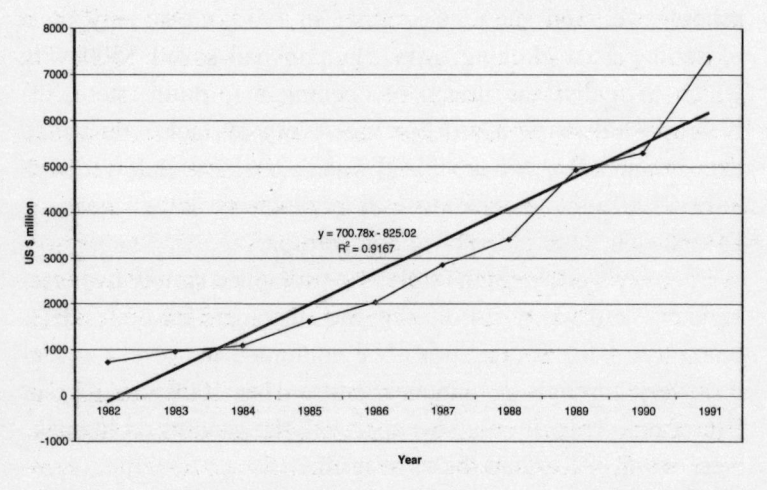

[Graph showing US $ million on y-axis (−1000 to 8000) vs Year on x-axis (1982–1991), with trend line equation $y = 700.78x - 825.02$ and $R^2 = 0.9167$]

Source: Adapted from data given in Berkshire Hathaway, *Letters to Shareholders*, 1982–1992

Had Buffet just struck lucky? Well, even looking at the graph suggests that his remarkable track record is down to something more than luck. Look at the trend line: it is steadily upwards, with a high correlation coefficient of 0.91. This indicates that fluctuations around the trend growth of US $700 million a year were fairly modest.

To get a more precise idea of whether Buffett's record is down to skill or luck, let's apply the Black Method to his stated 1984 goal of "maximising the average annual rate of gain in intrinsic business value on a per share basis." During the 1980s,

Buffet unquestionably succeeded in achieving his goal. The average annual rate of gain in Berkshire Hathaway's equity value was 31%. The standard deviation around this rate of gain was less than 14%, and the standard error just 4.6%, generating a t-statistic of almost 7 (31 divided by 4.6).

Even a t-statistic of 3 would imply a 99% probability that these results were due to something more than chance. With a t-statistic of 7, we can conclude beyond reasonable doubt that Buffett had a winning system for picking stocks.

Setting a tougher test – benchmarking Berkshire Hathaway against the average return of 12% per annum achieved on Wall Street as a whole – makes little difference to this conclusion. The *excess* return of Berkshire Hathaway over the Wall Street average was 19%, again with a standard error of 4.6%, generating the conclusion that we can be 99.9% confident that Buffet could beat Wall Street.

Buffet stands as a living indictment of the Efficient Market Hypothesis, which declares that financial markets efficiently discount all available information, so that they cannot be systematically beaten by careful stock selection.

Based on his record in the 1980s, an investor could have backed him with confidence into the 1990s, knowing that there was an extremely good chance that Buffet would continue to beat the market. Such an investor would not have been disappointed. Whilst Berkshire Hathaway's growth in the 1990s was somewhat slower than in the previous decade, it was still well ahead of the market. By 1999, Berkshire Hathaway's net worth had grown to more than $60 billion – over a hundred times more than in 1982 – and Buffet was able to report in his *Letter to Shareholders* on March 1st 1999 that "over the last 34 years since present management took over, per-share book value has grown from $19 to $37,801, a rate of 24.7% compounded annually."

Sadly, I was far too young to be in a position to invest $19 in Berkshire Hathaway 34 years ago.

Case 2 – The Rugby Tipster

The second case involves the bet recommendations made by Mike Nevin, *Odds On* rugby columnist, in his monthly articles published in the magazine between 1997 and 2000. Figure 19.2 summarises the column's overall results for those three seasons. Anyone following each of his recommendations over a period would have made a total profit of 288 units from 42 bets. But how confident can we be that this was not the result of chance?

The answer that immediately emerges from a visual inspection of Figure 19.2 is that we can be rather less confident of the system's viability than in the case of Berkshire Hathaway.

Although overall the column is well ahead, Figure 19.2 reveals that it has by no means been a smooth ride. In fact, it has been something of a rollercoaster, with profitable 1997/98 and 1999/2000 seasons punctuated by a poor season in 1998/99. Visually, it can be seen that fluctuations around the trend were much greater than in the case of Berkshire Hathaway.

Applying my method, it turns out that the average win from each of the 42 bets placed was 6.9 units. The standard deviation, or the extent to which actual results fluctuated away from the average, was no less than 37 units per bet. The standard error, equivalent to the standard deviation divided by the square root of the number of bets placed, was 5.7. Dividing the average result by the standard error to arrive at the t-statistic gives a figure of 1.2 (= 6.9 divided by 5.7).

Figure 19.2
Odds On Rugby Column. Record of Bet Recommendations, 1997–2000

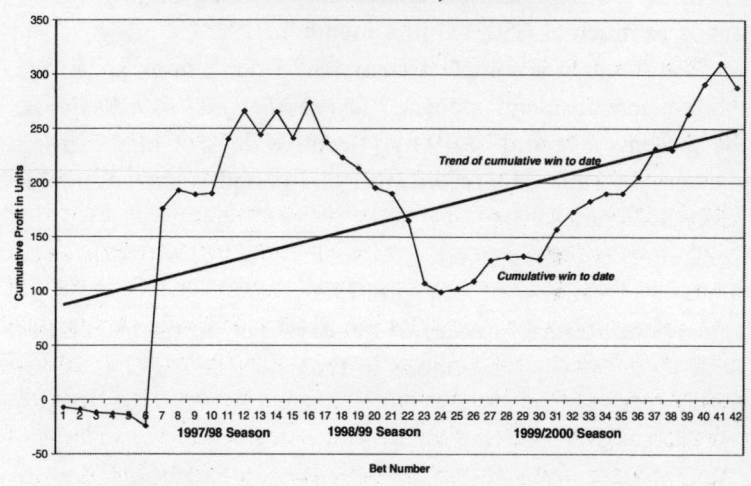

Source: Reproduced from *Odds On* Magazine, Issue No 96, July 2000

With a t-statistic of 1.2, there is approximately a 85% probability that the profits made by the *Odds On* rugby column over the three seasons were the result of skill. There is about a 15% chance that the column's success is down to nothing more than a temporary run of good fortune. Still, an 85% degree of confidence is pretty good, suggesting that the odds are about 6/1 on in favour of the conclusion that the column's successful record is due to skill rather than luck.

Case 3 – The Blackjack Player

In the 1950s and early 1960s, professional blackjack player Lawrence Revere made a fortune playing blackjack in the casinos of Nevada and the Caribbean. Talking about the game in the late 1960s, he commented that "There is more money to be made playing blackjack than doing anything I know. I have made as much as $50,000 in a month."

Was the man a complete charlatan? I don't think so. In the book where his claim appears, *Playing Blackjack as a Business*, he presents a record of 190 consecutive days of play starting January 1st 1963. His record over that period is shown graphically in Figure 19.3.

Figure 19.3
Lawrence Revere's Record of 190 days' play at the blackjack tables in 1963

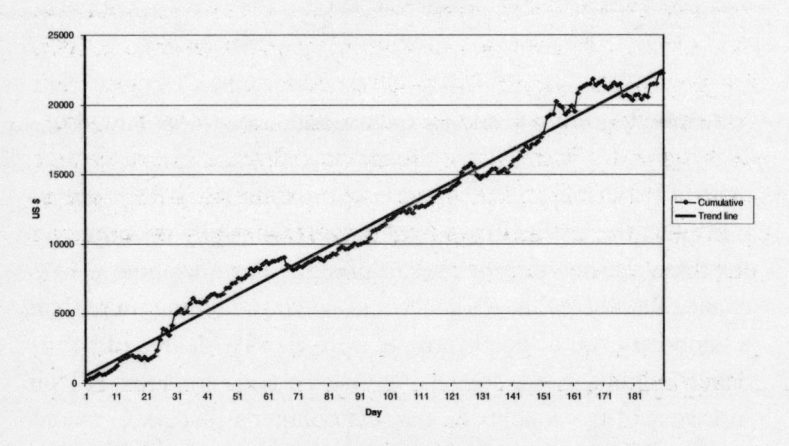

Source: Adapted from Playing Blackjack as a Business, Revised Edition 1980, p. 141

Revere's record indicates that, over the period, he won on 143 days, lost on 47 days, and made a total profit of $22,265 during the first six months of 1963, averaging a win of just under $120 per day. You could multiply this sum by around five to get the value in today's money. The standard deviation of his daily win was in excess of $200, but because of the large number of days he played, the standard error was less than $40. So Revere's daily win of $120 was more than four times the standard error of the daily win. Statistically, it is more than 99.9 per cent probable that he had a genuinely winning system; there is less than a 0.1 per cent chance that the results were down to luck.

But before you rush out to the nearest casino hoping to repeat Revere's feat, I should advise you that the game of blackjack has changed beyond recognition since the halcyon days of the early 1960s when he played. As Revere said, playing against a single deck game where the player was offered plenty of options on how to play the cards was an easy way to make money. But that was back in 1963. In the years since Revere passed on to that great card table in the sky, things have become a little tougher for the player. No more doubling down on any card; no resplitting of pairs; and, crucially, no more single- or double-deck games. These days, the game offered in most British casinos is dealt from a six-deck shoe, and impossible to beat as a practical proposition using the card counting methods employed by Lawrence Revere.

Conclusions

Anyone planning to make money out of their speculative activities needs to know when their systems are genuinely viable, and when they should cut their losses.

Amateur punters have little idea of the viability of the systems they are using. They play their hunches, are happy when they win, and soon forget about their losses. The professional speculator keeps a record of all wins and losses, regularly reviews progress, bets more when ahead, and is prepared to cut losses when a particular approach is clearly not working.

The professional approach can be reinforced by periodically assessing the effectiveness of particular systems. Using the methods set out in this chapter, you don't need to place a lot of bets before getting an idea of whether you are winning through luck or skill. We have established that Buffet's investment approach is highly effective on the basis of just ten observations. Even with a more volatile pattern of wins and losses, such as that experienced by the *Odds On* rugby column, we can start having a degree of confidence after 30 or 40 bets. If you're not reasonably confident that a particular system is profitable after this number of bets, it is probably not viable, and should be abandoned in favour of something better.

20

How to win at football betting

As I take up my pen to write this final chapter, I can only echo the words of Sky Masterson's father to his son as he embarked on his journey in life. "You are now going out into the wide, wide world to make your own way, and it is a very good thing to do," said the old man. "I am only sorry that I am unable to bankroll you to a very large start, but I am now going to stake you to some very valuable advice."

This advice is not how to apply specific formulae or systems that you can use to make money from the game. Sadly, any advice that I might offer of this type would be obsolete the moment it was published, because if I were to point out ways in which the betting market for football was inefficient, then the moment it was in the public domain it would be taken on board by the market makers and any betting opportunities that had existed would soon disappear.

So what is offered is a general method for winning at football betting, based on years of hard experience and research. The method has seven steps.

Step 1: Developing a forecasting model

Step 1 involves developing models to forecast the likely results of whichever market you wish to bet on. For example, the statistical methods discussed in Chapters 14 and 15 might form the basis for models to predict the probability of home wins or supremacy margins; or the type of approach described in Chapters 7 and 8 might form the basis for forecasts of tournament goalscoring patterns.

Incidentally, the forecasting method adopted may not be based exclusively on statistical analysis. You could adjust any statistical forecasts to take account of the sort of motivational factors described in Chapter 16, or apply a knowledge of the gambling biases discussed in Chapter 17 to gain an edge over the rest of the market. Perhaps best of all in this age of online gambling and betting in running is to use the evidence of your own eyes, watching a game live as it unfolds, to predict which side will win, how many goals will be scored, and even how many bookings are likely in the light of what is happening on the field.

Certainly, if you can read a game accurately as it is played, you stand to make a fortune from betting on football.

Step 2: Testing the model

Before you bet your house on your forecasts, it is advisable to test them first. If, over a series of 20 or 30 games, it turns out that your forecasts on a particular market, written down at the time that they were made, were a reasonable forecast of the actual results, then you may have a winning system on your hands. Clearly you will never be 100 cent accurate in any forecast you may make; but if the *average* forecast is close to the average results, and if any variances are randomly distributed around that average, then it suggests that, overall, whatever model you are using is reliable.

Testing your system may show up biases that you can correct – for example, a tendency to overestimate the favourite's supremacy, or the total number of goals likely to be scored, or an unconscious tendency to favour certain teams over others. If you do identify biases in your tests, you can correct them before the system goes live. As an old army friend of mine used to say, "time spent in reconnaissance is rarely wasted."

Step 3: Generating Prices

Once you have tested your model to the point where you have confidence in it, it is time to go live, by using it to generate real forecasts and odds. Any forecast that you make using the model should be written down at the time you make it, and before going on to Step 4.

Step 4: Shopping Around

As was emphasised in Chapter 11, for anyone serious about making money from football betting, shopping around is not an optional extra but a vital necessity. Only by getting the best prices on offer will you maximise your profits; and often you will not secure viable betting opportunities unless you get the best prices on offer. Viable bets only arise when your forecast differs from that of the bookmakers to a significant degree. On many occasions when my forecasts were significantly different from those of the bookies, the actual results fell somewhere between the two. I believe that the reason is that the bookmakers often take account of factors of which I am unaware, such as late player injuries, and adjust their lines accordingly. In such situations, if you simply accepted the average price quoted by bookmaking firms, or bet with the first firm you contacted, you will almost always win less than you could have, and often end up as a loser, quite unnecessarily. Over a long series of bets, minor differences in price can add up to many thousands of pounds.

Step 5: Placing the Bet

Having found the best available price, make sure that you are trading within the limits of your betting bank. As a rule of thumb, I aim to place no more than 5% to 10% of my speculative capital at risk on any single position, no matter how confident I am that the bet represents sound value. I'm equally prudent in my estimation of risk exposure, particularly on open-ended spread bets. My estimates are based on the worst possible outcome, not an average negative swing. So, for example, if I was selling Total Goals in a single game at, say, 2.5, then the worst case for me is not a 5-goal make-up but 8 or 9. There may only be a 1 in 100 chance of this number of goals being scored in the match, but sooner or later it will happen, and the bankroll must be capable of comfortably absorbing this level of loss. So playing off a £10,000 bankroll, a maximum 10% liability on any game would stipulate a maximum exposure of no more than £1,000. Selling goals at 2.5 and accepting a worst case of 9 goals would imply a maximum bet per goal of £1,000 divided by 6.5 (9 minus 2.5), which equates to approximately £150 per goal.

Step 6: Record results and measure progress

Whatever the outcome of a particular bet, you should always measure the results and record the win or loss. This is harder to do for losing bets than for winning bets, but it is an essential discipline for anyone who aspires to be a successful speculator. Records form the basis of measurement, and it is imperative to measure the success of any system used, applying methods such as those set out in Chapter 19 to establish when a system is making money and when it should be abandoned.

Step 7: Evaluation

The final step is to periodically review progress, and evaluate whatever systems you are using. A general rule of successful speculation is to "cut your losses, and let your profits run". Cutting losses may not involve abandoning a system altogether, but certainly if you are experiencing a steady haemorrhage of cash, you could be well advised to consider radical surgery before going on to place any further bets. Persevering with a profitable system is much easier, but even here periodic reviews may enhance the results.

Successful speculation is a process of continuous improvement, where the gambler follows the aspiration of Tennyson's Ulysses,

> *To follow knowledge like a sinking star*
> *Beyond the utmost bound of human thought.*

If, like me, you enjoy taking calculated risks and regard risk taking as essential to innovation and progress, then you will also know that occasional setbacks are inevitable. Provided that our exposure to loss is kept within manageable limits, losses can be positively beneficial in teaching us something more about ourselves and about the games on which we speculate, enabling us to generate greater profits in the future.

These days, I probably bet on most football matches that I watch, using my reading of the game to assess which team is on top and by how many goals they may win. My bets are not always successful, but they always have the effect of leading me to watch the game with a keener eye, learning something more from each phase of play and building up a store of knowledge that may be useful in the future. On those occasions when I do suffer losses, I am reminded of the closing words of *Ulysses*,

Tho' much is taken, much abides; and tho'
We are not now that strength which in old days
Moved earth and heaven; that which we are, we are,
One equal temper of heroic hearts,
Made weak by time and fate, but strong in will
To strive, to seek, to find, and not to yield.

What the Reviewers said

Spread Betting to Win

"Spread betting is far more technical and involved than fixed-odds betting. Fixed odds comes from the Stone Age, spread betting from the computer age. If you are going to dabble you need a good text book. One of the best is *Spread Betting to Win* by Jacques Black. Black's name is a pseudonym for a financial consultant who happens to be an expert on gambling. His book answers almost all the questions."
– *Financial Times*, November 27th / 28th 1999

"The author, who goes under the pseudonym Jacques Black and who has been banned from most London casinos for card counting, has written this book for the 'serious speculator' and concludes with eight golden rules of successful spread betting. We give this book a three-star rating."
– *Rugby World*, September 1999

"*Spread Betting to Win* by Jacques Black is aimed at the lay person and experienced punter which gives independent advice on how you can exploit the many advantages of spread betting. It covers such topics as why spread betting is so superior to fixed-odds betting as a speculative medium, how to open an account and start trading, how to manage your risks, how to play the spreads on financial markets, the eight golden rules of spread betting, and much more."

– *Betting Shop Magazine*, September 1998

"Perhaps ever since sports spread betting began, there have been claims that no definitive work – no easy-to-read, informative guide – existed to help those wanting to know more about this rapid growth area. Now, suddenly, there are two – *Spread Betting*, by Andrew Burke, and *Spread Betting to Win*, by Jacques Black. Whereas Burke is educating novice spread players in easy stages, Black is keener on discussing strategy as it affects high rollers. Black is well-versed in the casino scene, and his earlier book on blackjack, *The Moneyspinners*, is a fascinating work. I acknowledged his reasoning on buying the Highest Partnership at 230 when England met Australia in the Ashes Series in 1994/95. This chapter, 'Running a Position', is very strong on when trading in running is a sound move."

– Ian Carnaby, 'Definitive Works', *Odds On*, August 1998

"A book worth every penny of its £7.99. Black quite often uses graphs and charts to illustrate markets and how they may be expected to move. He provides a simple staking plan for risk management. Most fascinating of all is the case study in betting arbitrage. Black does not recommend playing two firms off against each other, but playing two totally separate markets. According to Black it was possible to virtually guarantee a profit by selling the total goals at 73 in Euro96, and hedge by selling the time of the fastest goal in the tournament. Unique insight into how to interpret value in different markets."

– *Racing Post,* August 26th 1998

"Author Jacques Black, a highly respected financial consultant, has aimed this 'how to' book at the full spectrum of gamblers, from the occasional flutterer to the regular punter, in order to help them overcome what he describes as the 'fear of the unknown.' Black is vastly experienced in this field of betting, and passes on his knowledge and tips for success to readers, including his eight golden rules of successful spread betting. He explains all aspects of spread betting – setting up an account, placing your first spread bet, the advantages and disadvantages of betting on different sports – as well as considering the fields of political and financial spread betting."

– *Investment Week*, June 8th 1998

"There is something here to please spread betting veterans, newcomers and those who are still at the 'thinking about it' stage. He has successfully combined the information of an instruction manual with an easy to read style. The main theme running through the book is an enthusiasm for spread betting tempered with the importance of risk management. Indeed Black never allows the reader to forget that they should build only from firm foundations. All in all, an excellent read, covering most of what you need to know about spread betting tactics."

– Stefan Perry, *SMARTSig Confidential*, June 1998

The Moneyspinners: How Professional Gamblers Beat the Casinos at their Own Game

"The pseudonymous author of this amusing and informative book on the mechanics, history and politics of gambling is at pains to disabuse us of one particular idea. That is: our cherished notion that today's professional card sharps resemble in any way the riverboat gamblers of old. These types are not flamboyant characters with ruffled shirts and pearl-handled revolvers stuck in their boot tops; rather they are men such as Lawrence Revere, who made a fortune playing blackjack and poker in Nevada and the casinos of the West Indies, who was deliberately and painstakingly inconspicuous, aiming to appear like an ordinary punter. The reason for this being the same as Jacques Black being a nom-de-plume. Namely, that if you reveal yourself to be a professional gambler in almost any casino in contemporary America or Britain, you will be barred."

– Will Self, *Sunday Times*, April 11 1993

"This book is a compulsive read. There are numerous historical vignettes (usually of spectacular and rare successes) which are something of a joy to behold. An epilogue extends gambling theory into other fields – offering a novel reading of the career of Margaret Thatcher. And various appendices will ensure that you will at least be very knowledgeable when you hit the streets."

– Frank Kuppner, *Glasgow Herald*, April 21 1993

"Black's speciality is blackjack, a game that requires mathematical talent and card-money as well as strategy. The most interesting parts of his book are his arguments in favour of equal rights for card-counters, the protection of compulsive gamblers against themselves, and his proposal that 'casinos should become places of entertainment where any two or more individuals may sit down together to challenge each other to a non-physical game of chance or skill played for money.' There are also interesting appendices on the mathematics of blackjack."

– Al Alvarez (author of *The Biggest Game in Town*), *Daily Mail*, April 29 1993

"Professional gamblers are prepared to lose thousands without flinching. They are unquestionably a people obsessed. Any book on the subject written by a professional cannot fail to be touched by that obsession . . . There is little doubt that 'Black' has not merely studied his methods with mathematical precision – as one might expect from his successes – he has also learnt from the ultimate practitioners of the art . . . *The Moneyspinners* does provide a revelatory insight into this powerful demi-monde."

– Tom Rhodes, *Times*, May 20 1993

"The only casino game that players can legitimately win is blackjack or twenty-one. *The Moneyspinners* rehearses in detail the experience of the experts in this field. *The Moneyspinners* draws judiciously on a variety of well-known gambling sources. Gambling in casinos yields great pleasure, but it is only when the player can deliberately turn the odds in his favour – by judgement and experience – that gambling becomes profitable. As far as straight casino gambling goes, there is no such thing as easy money."

– David Spanier (author of *Easy Money: Inside the Gambler's Mind*), Independent, May 20 1993

"Jacques Black has frequented the world's gaming watering

holes and knows a thing or two about gaming in general. So good is he at Blackjack that he has been barred from most London casinos for card counting. What is more, his scenario of scams and characters unfolds with the deadpan facts that comprise a fascinating read."

– Robin Lloyd, *Odds On*, July 1993

"Jacques Black was for a short spell the scourge of London casinos. Recognising quickly that roulette promised only poverty, Black became a blackjack king. He mastered the difficult art of card-counting, regarded by casino bosses as modern-day necromancy, and made a comfortable, if anti-social living. *The Moneyspinners* is a terrific read. It quickly delivers the bad news – that long term we haven't a hope in hell of winning at roulette – but softens the blow with the sweetener that it is possible to make blackjack pay. The only snag is you've got to be dedicated; you've got to be determined; and you've got to be damned clever. Card-counting is the key, but camouflage is also critical . . . Black certainly knows his stuff and his book is essential reading for anyone trying to make casino betting pay."

– Derek McGovern (Sports Editor), *Racing Post*, March 7 1994

Spread Betting to Win and *The Moneyspinners* are both available from Oldcastle Books, price £7.99 paperback

Bibliography

Deloitte & Touche, *Annual Review of Football Finance*, August 2000

Drapkin, Tony & Forsyth, Richard, *The Punter's Revenge: Computers in the World of gambling*, Chapman & Hall/Methuen, 1987

Elo, Arpad, *The Rating of Chess Players, Past and Present*, Batsford, 1978

Revere, Lawrence, *Playing Blackjack as a Business*, Lyle Stuart Inc, 1981

Sharpe, Graham, *Gambling on Goals: A Century of Football Betting*, Mainstream Publishing, 1997

Wagenaar, Willem A., *Paradoxes of Gambling Behaviour*, Lawrence Erlbaum Associates Ltd, 1988

Wright, Howard, *Bull: The Biography*, Timeform/Portway Press Ltd, 1995

David Jackson and K.R. Mosurski's paper on "Index Betting on Sports" cited in Chapter 14 is published in *Gambling and Commercial Gaming*, edited by William R. Eadington & Judy A. Cornelius, Institute for the Study of Gambling & Commercial Gaming, University of Nevada, Reno, 1992

The book also cited articles published in two monthly magazines:
Odds On (editor: Mark Crellin), Rowton Press Ltd, PO Box 10, Oswestry, Shropshire SY10 8WU
SMARTSig (editor: Stefan Perry), PO Box 44, Hayle TR27 6YH